A
Short History
of Africa

Other Pocket Essentials by this author:

A Short History of Europe

A
Short History
of Africa

From the Origins of the Human Race
to the Arab Spring

GORDON KERR

POCKET ESSENTIALS

First published in 2012 by Pocket Essentials,
an imprint of Oldcastle Books Ltd,
P.O.Box 394,
Harpenden, Herts, AL5 1XJ
www.pocketessentials.com

A CIP catalogue record for this book is available from the British Library.

ISBN
978–1–84243–442–0 (print)
978–1–84243–633–2 (kindle)
978–1–84243–634–9 (epub)
978–1–84243–635–6 (pdf)

4 6 8 10 9 7 5 3

Typeset by Avocet Typeset, Chilton, Aylesbury, Bucks, HP18 9FG
in 9pt Univers Light
Printed in Great Britain by CPI Group (UK) Ltd, Croydon, CR0 4YY

Contents

Introduction

Africa presents the historian with many interesting challenges. Not the least of them is its sheer size. The world's second-largest continent, at around 11.7 million square miles, it covers more than 20 per cent of the earth's total land area. With fifty four recognised sovereign states, bordered by the Mediterranean in the north, the Atlantic in the west and the Indian Ocean, and the Arabian and Red Seas in the east, it offers a sometimes confusing abundance of different peoples, ethnicities, societies and religions. Its geography, too, is diverse but, without understanding Africa's geography, one cannot possibly understand its history. Divided by the equator, forty per cent of its landmass is desert with the Sahara Desert its largest, stretching across North Africa, through a dozen countries, and spanning almost 3.5 million square miles.

We have a perception – probably derived from films and literature – of an Africa that is covered by dense forest, but impenetrable tropical rainforest takes up only eight per cent of the continent. The remainder is comprised of Sahel – a thousand mile-wide, coast-to-coast buffer zone between the desert in the north and the savannah and wooded grasslands of the south. Numerous mountain ranges reach up into Africa's skies, from the Atlas range in the north, which extends across Morocco, Algeria and Tunisia, to the Drakensberg range in southern Africa. Its rivers cut dramatic gorges and plummet over spectacular waterfalls such as Victoria Falls (known to Africans as Mosi-oa-Tunya), while its beautiful lakes ripple into the distance. The biggest, Lake Victoria Nyanza, which borders Uganda, Kenya and Tanzania, is the second-largest lake in the world at 26,560 square miles.

Making sense of such social and geographical diversity is not helped by the lack of written resources. But, of course, although African societies of the past were non-literate, that does not render their history any less fascinating than the well-chronicled histories of the nations of the western world. And thanks to anthropologists, archaeologists and linguists, we have uncovered the stories of Africa's past, the movements of its peoples, its empires, its kingdoms and its great men and women.

In 1871, when Charles Darwin suggested in *The Descent of Man*, that the birthplace of mankind was, in all likelihood, located in Africa, Europeans were horrified. It was not just that he was overturning the Biblical notion that in seven days God had created the earth and all the creatures that inhabited it – although that, in itself, proved controversial enough – it was also the fact that he was going against the presumption that Europeans were superior to the world's other races and promoting the idea – absurd to Victorian ears – that their progenitors were Africans. Research in the twentieth century and from the 1950s onwards in particular, has, however, provided ample evidence to support Darwin's claim that Africa is, indeed, the 'cradle of humankind'.

But, despite its auspicious beginnings, Africa has, for too long, been no more than a warehouse for the rest of the world, a source of free labour and precious minerals and there is a danger that it will continue to be so, as the world's great powers vie for the riches that lie beneath African soil in a 'new scramble for Africa'. One can only hope that this will not come to pass and that this vibrant, exciting continent will continue to enhance the world with its people, its beauty and its colourful history.

Prehistoric Africa

In 1924, in a limestone cave near Taung, in South Africa's Cape Province, anthropologist Raymond Dart discovered the skull of a six-year-old creature which he named *Australopithecus* ('southern ape'). Although ape-like, *Australopithecus* exhibited human characteristics and had walked upright on two legs with a slight stoop. It was small, only about 1.25 metres tall and would have weighed around twenty five kilos. Its teeth, approximating those of a human, had adapted to eating meat as well as vegetables. Critically, however, the brain of *Australopithecus* would have been substantially larger than that of an ape. Emerging around four million years ago, *Australopithecus* became extinct two million years later.

The brain capacity of *Australopithecus* was somewhere between 440 and 500cc but hominid skulls discovered in the Olduvai Gorge and near Lake Turkana in Kenya's Great Rift Valley exhibit brain capacities of between 650 and 800cc. With this creature, known as *Homo habilis* ('handy' man), who lived 2.3 to 1.4 million years ago at the beginning of the Pleistocene period, were found simple stone tools. *Homo habilis* was followed by *Homo erectus* who fashioned the hand axe, a stone implement with more regular and consistent flaking on each face than had been hitherto produced. By around 40,000 BC, the next version of the *Homo* genus, *Homo sapiens*, had evolved into *Homo sapiens sapiens*, modern humans, with a brain capacity of about 1,400cc. Within 30,000 years, this version had spread from its African origins and colonised the world.

It was the manufacture of stone tools that set the *Homo* line apart from other animals. This took place during the era known as the 'Stone Age', the prehistoric period lasting about two and a half million years immediately preceding the discovery of metals around 6,000 years ago. Stone implements with sharp, pointed or percussive surfaces were manufactured. It was with the arrival of *Homo erectus*, around one and a half million years ago, that a dramatic technological advance was made. The hand axe, usually known as 'Acheulian', from Saint-Acheul, the location in southern France where it was first discovered, was the first tool to be crafted to a pre-determined shape. These people were also the first to use fire for cooking as well as for warmth.

The Middle Stone Age, dating from about 150,000 years ago, brought the emergence of *Homo sapiens*. Bone began to be used and stone tools grew ever more sophisticated. During the second phase of the Middle Stone Age, stone pieces began to be fitted onto a length of wood or other material. Around this time, climatic changes affected food supply and it is possible that an increased population led to people seeking better ways to exploit their environment. This led in turn to regional specialisation. The peoples of the more sparsely wooded areas of the savannah hunted game with spears whilst the inhabitants of the wetter and more thickly forested regions lived by collecting fruit and vegetables as well as by fishing.

The Later Stone Age brought *Homo sapiens sapiens* who evolved from around 40,000 years ago. He started to carve the microlith – small stone flakes shaped into blades and arrow- and spear-heads, making hunting more efficient. People lived in camps in open country beside lakes or streams. Rock shelters or caves, often decorated with paintings of animals and hunting scenes, were also commonly used.

Around 10,000 years ago there was another immense step forward when humans began to domesticate animals and cultivate crops, such as wheat, barley, sorghum and millet. This encouraged them to settle longer in one place, leading to more permanent shelters, constructed from mud or bricks. Stability led to a rapid increase in population, necessitating a greater degree of organisation and cooperation in the planning of agricultural activities.

Farming was long thought to have first developed in Mesopotamia (modern Lebanon, Syria, south-eastern Turkey, Iraq and western Iran), the area known as the 'Fertile Crescent', but it is now believed to have actually developed in a number of different parts of the world around the same time. In Africa, it probably did not develop in isolation. There was a great deal of communication between the different regions as well as with Asia from where, in exchange for a number of domesticated plant species such as sorghum, Africa received other cereals – wheat and barley, for instance. Bananas, the greater yam and the taro came from southern Arabia via the east African coast.

Tropical cereal farming became widespread in the savannah grasslands on the southern edges of what is now the Sahara desert where, between 8,000 and 4,000 BC, the climate was wetter than today. Fishing communities had established themselves around rivers and lakes from the upper Niger Delta in the west to Lake Chad, the Upper Nile, Lake Turkana and the Great Rift Valley in the east. As the climate became drier in these areas, however, and the Sahara encroached on their lands, they were forced to resort to domesticating a number of tropical African cereals. During the next three millennia, the cultivation of sorghum and millet spread from Senegambia in the west to the Upper Nile in the east and Neolithic farming practices continued to spread through the tropical forest zones.

In the Ethiopian highlands, people developed their own distinctive crops, including *tef*, a cereal that remains a staple in the area to this day. Pastoralism was predominant in Uganda and northern Kenya, although some cereals were also being cultivated. Meanwhile, the peoples south of the equator remained hunter-gatherers until the start of the Iron Age, two thousand years ago.

The keeping of cattle, sheep and goats dates back in northern Africa as far as 7,000 BC and, in the savannah grasslands of the central and northern Sahara, pastoralism appears to have been more important than crop cultivation. A significant factor in its spread was the presence or absence of the blood-sucking tsetse fly which carries in its saliva the parasite that causes 'sleeping sickness' in both humans and cattle. Immunity would eventually develop in humans who moved into a tsetse-infected area, but, on the whole, such areas were to be avoided by pastoralists. As tsetse were most common in damper, low-lying valleys and wooded areas, pastoralism thrived on the drier and more open savannah grasslands of the southern plateaux. Domesticated cattle bones found in the Great Rift Valley and Serengeti plains of East Africa date to around 5,000 BC and pastoralism was well established by 2,000 BC while, in southern Africa, it seems to have spread as far as the extreme south west by the last couple of centuries BC.

Agriculture – as well as warfare – was transformed by another vital discovery – iron-smelting. There is evidence that it developed independently in East and West Africa but the technology was almost certainly imported from southwest Asia. The first type of furnace used for melting iron ore in sub-Saharan Africa was a primitive trench or bowl, but this was later replaced by beehive-shaped kilns or more efficient cylindrical structures in which the temperature could be raised with bellows to more than 2,000 degrees. These distinctive furnaces were different to anything seen in North Africa, Mesopotamia or the Maghreb, casting doubt on the theory that the technology arrived in sub-Saharan Africa by way of the Mediterranean and the desert.

Its rapid spread across the continent gave Africans the tools with which to advance their societies. They now had the hoe to clear land for settlement and cultivation, rendering the thick forest less impenetrable. They also had the weapons to make hunting more efficient. Farming became more intensive and productive, allowing people to move from subsistence farming to the production of surpluses. This meant that communities could trade with neighbours with a different speciality. Critically, however, it also enabled them to support classes of people not specifically involved in food production – specialist craftsmen, religious officials, administrators and rulers. Thus did the gap between rich and poor in society begin, non-producers becoming wealthy and the actual producers of the food on which everyone lived remaining poor.

It was the beginning of civilisation as we know it.

Ancient Civilisations and Medieval States

Ancient Egypt, 3,100–332 BC

The Nile valley is uniquely positioned, not only for access to the African regions bordering it, but also to distant centres of ancient civilisation such as those of the Arabian Peninsula, the Indian Ocean and the Mediterranean. It also provided unique challenges and opportunities for the people living there. The River Nile is fed by the White Nile, the Blue Nile and the Atbara. The White Nile enables a regular flow of water in the lower Nile but, following the summer rains in the Highlands of Ethiopia where they originate, the Blue Nile and the Atbara are transformed into raging torrents that carry the dark, fertile soils of the highlands down into the Nile's lower valley. Every August, the river burst its banks and flooded the narrow valley located on either bank, depositing rich soil in which seeds could be planted and harvested. Around 5,000 to 4,000 BC, permanent settlements established themselves along the banks of the river, adapting their agricultural techniques to its annual flood.

Homo sapiens had already been living in the area of the Nile as early as the Palaeolithic Era, the population fluctuating with environmental and climatic changes. It is impossible to determine to which race these people belonged, just as it has long been a matter of debate whether Ancient Egyptians were black- or white-skinned. Indeed, it may be safest to conclude that they were not a people of one pure race, but a mixture of peoples on the move not only from Africa but the Middle East and even Europe.

As the Neolithic Age came to an end, sometime between 3,300 and 2,400 BC, the climate of the Sahara grew drier, forcing people to move themselves and their livestock eastwards to the Nile valley. Sacral – semi-divine – chiefdoms emerged which became increasingly powerful as the increase in population led to competition for farmland, creating a need for regulation. Bureaucracies began to form amongst the chiefdoms. By late in the fourth millennium BC, the long strip of arable land beside the Nile was supporting around 1.8 million people, heralding the beginning of one of the world's greatest and longest-lasting civilisations.

Egypt became a unified state when the chiefdoms of Upper and Lower Egypt were united under the rule of the first Pharaoh, Narmer (also known as Menes), who represented the first of thirty ruling dynasties that remained in power until 332 BC, a span of 2,768 years. This great civilisation would leave behind a legacy of extraordinary temples and tombs and would make huge advances in scientific pursuits such as navigation, astronomy and medicine. Amongst their greatest achievements was the development of hieroglyphics, one of the world's earliest forms of writing. Mainly inscribed on papyrus – an ancient type of paper made from the pith of the papyrus plant – or on stone, it consisted of a series of images each of which represented a sound or had a meaning.

The majority of Egyptian people were poor peasant farmers living in mud houses built above the flood plain. They grew wheat, barley and flax as well as a range of vegetables and fruit and they reared goats and cattle. They ate little meat as most of it went in taxes to be enjoyed by the wealthy ruling classes. The surplus they produced from their fields also went to the tax collector, leaving them just enough to survive until the next harvest. Government control was stringent, exploitative and inescapable. The Pharaoh sat at the top of a rigid hierarchy, below him the priests, scribes and large numbers of civil servants responsible for assessing and collecting taxes. At the bottom were the peasants who worked the land but were regularly conscripted to work on communal projects such as irrigation and marsh-draining, as well as the construction of temples and royal tombs such as the Great Pyramid at Giza.

The Pharaohs were seen as gods on earth, at the head of a religious system that involved the worship of a number of deities amongst whom were Osiris, king of the dead and the sun god, Ra, from whom the Pharaohs claimed descent. Burial rites were of huge importance, particularly as Egyptians believed in life after death and reincarnation. The bodies of the rich and powerful dead were, therefore, embalmed and mummified in order to preserve them. Food was buried with them as well as offerings that might prove useful in the afterlife. During the Fourth Dynasty (c. 2,620–2,494 BC), the Egyptians began long-distance trading, importing, amongst other things, timber from the Levant and gold and skins from Nubia.

Until they were conquered in 332 BC by Alexander the Great of Macedonia, Egyptians experienced a remarkable three millennia of relative stability, made possible by their own conservatism and by the deserts on either side of the Nile that were a deterrent to potential invaders.

Nubia and the Kingdoms of Kush and Meroe; 806 BC–350 AD

Situated in the area of modern southern Egypt and northern Sudan, Nubia enjoyed a complex relationship with its powerful northern neighbour. When Egypt was stable and strong, it plundered Nubia for gold and slaves; when it was weak from internal strife or invasions, it traded amicably with the Nubians. During the New Kingdom (c. 1,550–1,070 BC), Nubia was annexed by Egypt for five centuries during which period the Nubians were deeply influenced by Egyptian culture and society. Nubians served as mercenaries in the Egyptian army where they were particularly renowned for their prowess as archers. When the New Kingdom slipped into decline, there was chaos in Egypt. Nubia, free of Egyptian domination, began to restore its own political, economic, cultural and social systems.

The Kingdom of Kush first came to notice in 760 BC when Kashta (ruled c. 760–752 BC) invaded Egypt and became the first Nubian Pharaoh, launching the Twenty fifth Dynasty and moving the capital to

Thebes. The conquest of Upper Egypt was completed in the reign of the following two Pharaohs, Piye (ruled c. 752–721 BC) and Shabaka (ruled c. 721–707 BC) who ruled a kingdom that stretched more than 2,000 miles along the Nile, from the fourth cataract to the Mediterranean.

In the following century, a new Asiatic threat emerged. The Assyrians, under King Esarhaddon (ruled 681–669 BC), defeated Pharaoh Taharqa (ruled 690–664 BC), and a few years later, the last Nubian Pharaoh, Tantamani (ruled 664–656 BC), fled back to Napata in Kush. His successors ruled over the Kingdom of Kush, as its inhabitants called it, for the next thousand years, initially from their capital at Napata but then, after an Egyptian attack around 500 BC, from Meroe. The move symbolically situated the Kushite kingdom closer to black Africa and African influence was evident in its society. The Kingdom of Meroe then developed independently of Egypt.

Kushite rulers were supported by a powerful army and an effective civil service. Like the Egyptian rulers, they depended upon the agricultural labours of their subjects. Egyptian gods were worshipped, but the Kushites gradually developed their own religion, architecture and culture. They grew their tropical cereals away from the banks of the Nile and their farms were spread over a wide area. They lived in villages governed by chiefs or heads of families and were not as rigidly ruled as their northern brethren. The country grew wealthy on its gold deposits and on its control of trade routes. An iron industry flourished with fuel for smelting the iron ore coming from the forests of the Butana plain. The official language of the kingdom was Meroitic, a Nilo-Saharan language, while Egyptian was Afro-Asiatic.

By 350 AD, however, Meroe was in serious decline. Environmental damage caused by over-exploitation of the land led to a fall in agricultural production. The making of huge quantities of charcoal for iron-smelting resulted in the exhaustion of forest resources. Furthermore, the decline in the fortunes of Rome led to a fall in demand for luxury goods from Meroe and the emergent kingdom of Axum stole a great deal of Meroe's trade via the Red Sea to the Indian

Ocean. Eventually, the Christian Ethiopian King Ezana of Axum (ruled c. 325–c. 360 AD) destroyed Meroe around 350 AD, bringing to an end twenty centuries of Nubia and the Kingdoms of Kush and Meroe.

The Rise and Fall of Axum, 200–700 AD

During the sixth century BC, hunters and traders from Saba (modern Yemen) in south-western Arabia began crossing the Red Sea to establish small trading settlements on the Eritrean coast of north-east Africa. These people, speaking the Sabaean language, had long exploited their fortuitous trading position between the Red Sea and the Indian Ocean and were now making the journey across the Red Sea in search of ivory to be traded with India and Persia. Experts in the skills of terracing and irrigation, they quickly realised the agricultural potential provided by the fertile valleys of Tigré and Amhara and, within a century, they had established colonies and were intermarrying with the indigenous population. Their language evolved into Ge'ez, the language from which Amharic, official tongue of the modern Federal Republic of Ethiopia, is descended. These speakers of Ge'ez mainly lived inland but established a successful port at Adulis on the coast, exploiting the Greek colonisation of Egypt and the Greek trade that was carried on through the Bab-el-Mandeb – the strait that led from the Red Sea to the Indian Ocean.

By the first century AD, the Sabaean colonists had established a powerful state at Axum that was independent of their Arabian homeland, and Adulis had become the most important ivory market in north-east Africa. As Axum grew, the initial racial divisions between the 'red' Sabaeans and the indigenous 'black' Cushitic pastoralists faded. By the first century AD, the inhabitants of Axum had evolved into the ancestors of the people who now call themselves Ethiopians. The zenith of Axum's empire was achieved in the fifth century by which time it was renowned throughout the world, from Rome to China. The city was home to a population of 20,000, and its elite flaunted their prosperity in grand houses and luxury goods. Axumites constructed tall, granite obelisks – or stelae – one hundred and forty of which have been discovered, although the majority have collapsed over the centuries.

King Ezana of Axum was converted to Christianity towards the end of his reign by the Syro-Phoenician Greek Frumentius (died c. 383 AD). Frumentius, who had been taken prisoner as a boy during a voyage to Ethiopia with his uncle and brother, travelled to Alexandria when he was old enough to be consecrated as a bishop. Returning to Ethiopia, he established his episcopal see at Axum, baptised King Ezana, built a number of churches and spread Christianity. He was the first *Abune*, the title given to the head of the Ethiopian church that was enjoyed by the 110 men who succeeded him during the next sixteen centuries until 1951 when the Church of Ethiopia became self-governing. There may have been pragmatic reasons for Ezana's conversion. He would have been eager to ingratiate himself and his country with his trading partners in the Greek-speaking eastern Mediterranean. It was, nonetheless, a significant moment in Ethiopian history.

The kings of Axum derived their wealth and power from taxes levied on the foreign trade entering and exiting Adulis but, as Islam gained ground across western Asia and northern Africa, Axum began to lose its trading relationships. To make matters worse, the Persian Gulf, rather than the Red Sea, became the preferred route for trade between the Indian Ocean and the eastern Mediterranean. The collapse of the Roman Empire as well as climate change further contributed to Axum's decline and, like the Kingdom of Kush, it also suffered from the over-exploitation of its soil. The chopping down of trees for iron smelting over many centuries created erosion that is still evident today. Adulis was destroyed by the Arabs in the eighth century and, by the ninth century, once-mighty Axum consisted of little more than a few villages and monasteries.

Greeks, Romans, Vandals and Byzantines: 323 BC–698 AD

Following the death of Alexander the Great in 323 BC, one of his generals, Ptolemy, was appointed *satrap* – governor – of Egypt.

Ptolemy founded a dynasty of Greek-speaking Pharaohs that ruled Egypt for the next two hundred and seventy five years, the Thirty Second and last Dynasty. Egypt was strategically critical to the Greeks, forming a link between the Mediterranean and the African interior and Indian Ocean. In order to exploit to the full the potential trading opportunities offered by possession of Egypt, Alexandria was founded on the Mediterranean coast of the Nile delta. Half a century later, an Egyptian trading fleet of some four thousand ships was carrying goods in both directions. The more fluid Greek writing supplanted hieroglyphics and a Greek-speaking bureaucracy governed the country, raising taxes that ultimately benefited the already wealthy merchants and the ruling elite.

By the end of the first century AD, the Roman Empire held sway in the Mediterranean, but in North Africa they encountered a formidable foe in the former Phoenician trading post of Carthage. Founded in 814 BC, within two hundred years Carthage had become wealthy and powerful on trade from sub-Saharan Africa. Salt was the principal item that was traded but, as time passed, other goods such as copper and gold were carried. Eventually, Carthage began to expand its territory in Africa, a policy associated with the Magonid family, led by Hanno (ruled 480–440 BC), son of Hamilcar (ruled 510–480 BC) who was described by the Greek writer Dio Chrysostom (c. 40–c. 120) as being responsible for 'transforming the Carthaginians from Tyrians into Africans'.

Carthage fought three significant wars with Rome. The First Punic War (264–241 BC), fought over Sicily, ended in defeat. In the Second Punic War (218–201 BC), the great military commander Hannibal (247–183 or 182 BC) invaded Europe and advanced on Rome. In 206 BC, however, Roman general Scipio Africanus (235–183 BC) invaded Africa. Recalled from Italy in 203 BC, Hannibal was defeated at Zama the following year. Carthage would last only another fifty years. The city was razed to the ground by a Roman army in 146 BC, bringing to an end the only power to resist her domination of the known world.

Rome did not assume control of North Africa for another century. They named their new province 'Africa', although the origins of the name are unclear. It may be derived from *Afri*, the name of semitic peoples who lived near Carthage. Another hypothesis states that it comes from a Berber word, *ifri*, meaning 'cave'. It has, of course, come to be used for the entire continent.

The Romans formed an alliance with the powerful Berber neighbours of Carthage, Numidia and Mauritania. But, within a couple of centuries, these regions had also become part of the Roman Empire. The agricultural resources of Rome's North African provinces were exploited to the full, and not for nothing was North Africa known as 'the granary of the empire'. Meanwhile, in Egypt, farmers were taxed even more heavily than during the time of the Pharaohs.

The indigenous Berbers of the Sahara, living outside Roman control, constantly attacked the empire's southern border. The Romans even introduced the camel to the region in order to achieve greater mobility, but the Berbers merely captured them and made life even more difficult for the Roman legions. Increasing urbanisation and the use of land for agriculture was damaging to Berber society and many Berbers were forced to settle or move away from lands on which they had lived for generations. Antagonism towards the Roman occupiers was, therefore, constant. The Emperor Trajan (ruled 98–117) built a line of defensive forts, establishing a southern frontier but, to the west, Roman authority did not extend inland until much later.

In 429 AD, an 80,000-strong force of the Germanic people known as the Vandals, crossed the Straits of Gibraltar under the leadership of their king, Genseric (ruled 428–477), and drove the Romans, who had already lost Numidia and Mauritania to the Berbers, from North Africa. Vandal control of North Africa was a prosperous period for the region. Trade and agriculture were maintained and the Vandal possessions became known as the 'grain empire'. From the south, however, they endured incursions by the Berbers. There were also religious problems, since the Vandals were Christian but were considered heretical by the Catholic Church. The clergy, therefore, suffered systematic repression and anti-Catholic feeling was prevalent.

To make matters worse, the men who succeeded Genseric proved to be incompetent and given to excesses. It took Byzantine general Belisarius (500–565) just three months to destroy Vandal authority in North Africa and regain the region for the Eastern Roman Empire. To the dismay of the population, the Byzantines returned the administration of the territory to the rigidly conservative structure of the past. The next hundred and fifty years were perpetually insecure. They sought to restore tax revenue to previous levels, reinstating the *annona*, an annual tax payable in wheat. Estates confiscated by the Vandals were returned to their previous owners but, despite the crushing tax burden, life was fairly prosperous, although it is doubtful if prosperity extended as far as the rural population.

Orthodox Catholicism was restored and the Arianism of the Vandals was proscribed, as was the Berber heresy of Donatism which held that people who had given up the Church during the persecutions of Roman Emperor Diocletian (ruled 284–305) should not be permitted to administer the sacraments. With administrative problems, military insubordination, corruption in the government and the constant Berber threat from the south, the end was fairly inevitable. It took the invading Arabs just fifty years – from 647 to 698 – to consign the Byzantine period in North Africa to history.

The Bantu Migrations, 1,000 BCE–1,600 CE

Languages evolve. This is especially evident when people move away from one another. As time passes, their once-common language adapts to circumstances and inter-mingling with other peoples. New words and phrases are coined and dialects emerge until eventually, although their languages are derived from the same family, the two sets of people no longer understand each other. By tracing the genealogy of languages, linguists can map the movement of people away from their original homeland.

This method has been used to follow the extensive migration of the Bantu people across large swathes of the African continent – Bantu Africa – that has resulted in 450 related languages that make up the Benue-Congo branch of the larger Niger-Congo family of languages.

The word root *ntu* is a common element of the languages of this family and means 'person'. The prefix *ban* indicates that it is plural. The word *bantu*, therefore, means 'people'. Such research has identified the homeland of the Bantu as being within an area between the modern day countries of Cameroon and Nigeria.

The migratory process, a slow dispersal of small groups, rather than an organised movement of people, took place over the course of centuries in the thousand years before the birth of Christ. Some Bantu travelled eastwards, along the northern edge of the equatorial rainforest to equatorial East Africa, the Congo, Uganda, Kenya and Tanzania. Meanwhile, others moved through the rainforest in a southerly direction before heading north-east to the coast of East Africa and south to central Africa and onwards to southern Africa where they eventually arrived in the sixteenth century. It is unknown what drove the Bantu migrants to leave; why others remained behind is also a mystery.

The Bantu people took with them the art of iron smelting, a technology that may have been brought to them by the Phoenicians who founded Carthage on the north coast of Africa in 800 BC or that may have traversed the Sahara with Berber nomads. Iron smelting may even have been discovered in Africa itself. None of these theories has been conclusively proved. What is certain is that, by about 500–400 BC, iron smelting was being practised in the modern areas of Nigeria, central Niger and southern Mali and by 1,000 AD other peoples of West Africa were using the technology. The Bantu would not have been able to produce great quantities of iron and what they produced were more likely to be farming implements – especially the hoe – which were used to clear forests and work the fertile soil of the savannah beyond the rainforest.

They worked a piece of land for two or three years until it was exhausted before abandoning it and moving on. But, as they moved in waves across the continent, the Bantu interacted with already established communities, intermarrying and trading with them. They brought their superior Iron Age weaponry and tools as well as social, political and cultural change:

'In some areas they brought notions of government, controlling people, development of leadership, chieftaincy, state-craft and organising people for campaigns for battles and also maybe a kind of advanced religion.'

Professor Leonard Ngcongco, University of Botswana

Nubian Christian States: 543 AD–1,500 AD

Following the collapse of the Kingdom of Kush in 350 BC, it split into three kingdoms – Nobatia, Makuria and Alwa. Makuria soon conquered Nobatia. Christianity first arrived in Nobatia in 543 AD and quickly spread to Makuria and Alwa but, for the Nobadian rulers, conversion was more about access to Christian Egypt and the Mediterranean than spirituality. Churches and cathedrals were built but the monastic tradition failed to take off in Nubia. Perhaps there was not the means to support a monastic community because the clergy were too busy making conversions to isolate themselves in monastic contemplation.

When the Persians invaded Egypt in 616, they stopped at the Nubian border, finally ending Nubia's relationship with Egypt and the supervision of the Nubian church by the patriarchate of Alexandria. In 641, Egypt came under Arab control and Christian Nubia was cut off from the Mediterranean for centuries.

For seven centuries, Nubia and the Arabs adhered to a treaty – the *Baqt* – which recognised Christian Nubia, mainly because of the strength of the Nubian army. Nonetheless, the Arabs still launched attacks on their southern neighbour. As a consequence of these skirmishes, northern and central Nubia united as far as the Alwa border under one king, possibly Merkurios (ruled 697–c. 722) of Makuria.

Eventually, by 1366, the Kingdom of Makuria had dissolved into petty chiefdoms and trade. Christianity and the ruling elite had vanished. The Muslims seized the opportunity to bring their faith to the Sudan and, by the fifteenth century, Arabs were living in Lower

Nubia, and formerly Christian Nubians were speaking Arabic and practising Islam. The collapse of Makuria allowed the Arabs to penetrate into Alwa which, by the sixteenth century, had disappeared.

Arabs and Islam

By the time of the death of the Prophet Muhammad in 632, almost all the Arabs of Arabia had accepted the Islamic faith. Islam brought unity to a people already linked by their common language, Arabic, giving them the strength to cast their gaze beyond Arabia to the wealth of the nations of Africa and beyond. Muhammad's message spread into North and East Africa and, in 639, the Arabs invaded Egypt, ruled at the time by the Eastern Roman Empire of Byzantium. Tired of corrupt, oppressive Byzantine rule, Egyptians welcomed them.

Conquest of the coastal region of North Africa to the west of Egypt – known to the Arabs as al-Maghreb ('the West') – proved difficult. The Egyptians had been glad to see the back of the Byzantines, but North African Berbers were more reluctant. Nonetheless, what is now Tunisia fell in 647, the city of Kairouan being founded in order to govern the new Muslim Arab province that was named 'Ifriqiya'.

Meanwhile, the Byzantines' powerful navy still operated in the area, protecting the re-built city of Carthage which the Byzantines had captured from the Vandals in 533. It took the Arabs until the 690s to establish a fleet large enough to defeat the Byzantines and Carthage then changed hands several times until 698 when Hasan ibn al-Nu'man (died c. 700) defeated the Byzantine emperor Tiberios III (ruled 698–705). Roman Carthage was destroyed and replaced by the city of Tunis, constructed by the Muslims nearby. The Byzantines subsequently withdrew almost entirely from Africa, remaining only in Ceuta, an important trading centre and a strategically vital city located across the Strait of Gibraltar from the

Iberian Peninsula and between the Mediterranean and the Atlantic. The Berber chiefdoms, meanwhile, made constant incursions into Ifriqiya from the west while, in the northern Sahara, the nomads remained a persistent problem. By 711, however, the Arabs had worn down Berber resistance and stood on the Atlantic coast of North Africa, hungrily eyeing Spain across the water. While the Arabs ruled along the Mediterranean coast as far as Ifriqiya, Arab-Berbers ruled the Maghreb al-Aqsa – the Far West (modern-day Morocco).

The Arabs gave their subject peoples a choice – they could pay a poll-tax, they could convert or they could die. Needless to say, the money brought in by taxation of non-Muslims proved extremely useful, freeing Muslims in the region from taxation. Understandably, there was no great desire for an all-out campaign of conversion. Within Egypt, the Arabs, like previous occupiers, saw the Nile Valley as a source of wealth and food but they were less oppressive than earlier rulers such as the Greeks and the Romans. They also re-introduced irrigation projects and improved agricultural production. As a result of the attractiveness of Muslims' tax-exempt status, plus the immigration of Arab peasants in the eighth and ninth centuries, Islam spread rapidly and, by the tenth century, Egypt as well as the Maghreb was Arabic-speaking and Muslim.

A number of politically independent Muslim Arab-Berber states would evolve in the coming centuries as the initial unity of the Arabs in North Africa began to crumble. North African Muslims began to assert their independence from the Caliphate – the central Islamic authority – which was helped in the ninth century by a dispute in the Islamic world over who was the successor to the Prophet. The fiercely independent Berbers, hostile to outside interference and to the Arab domination of orthodox Islam, embraced the unorthodox Shi'ite and Kharijite Islamic doctrines. Kharijite kingdoms came and went in the eighth and ninth centuries and, in the early tenth century, Syrian Shi'ites who claimed descent from Muhammad's daughter Fatima established the Fatimid Dynasty in the Maghreb. By 965, they ruled the entire region and, four years later, Egypt was also under their control. From 959 to 1171, the Fatimids ruled North Africa from Egypt to Morocco.

Espousing orthodox Sunnism and aspiring to a purer version of Islam, Abdallah ibn Yasin (d. 1059) founded the Almoravid Empire (1054–1147) that extended from the Sahel eastwards to the Mediterranean. In 1061, two years after his death, his brother, Abu Bakr ibn-Umar (d. 1087), replaced him, but was usurped by Yusuf ibn Tashfin (ruled c. 1061–1106). Abu Bakr returned to the Sahara where he continued the conflict with the Soninke. Yusuf ibn Tashfin, meanwhile, eventually crossed the Mediterranean to conquer southern Spain.

In the eleventh century, the Banu Hilal arrived in North Africa. These nomadic, warrior Arabs were unleashed on the Maghreb by the Fatimid caliph, Abu Tamim al-Mustansir (ruled 1036–1094), in order to rid Egypt of their unruly behaviour. Their arrival was a major factor in the Arabisation of the Maghreb and in the spread of nomadism into areas where agriculture had been predominant. In 1145, the Zenata Berber, Abd al-Mu'min (1094–1163) overthrew the corrupt Almoravids, founding the fundamentalist Almohad Empire (1145–1269) which treated non-Muslims harshly, forcing many Christians and Jews to emigrate. Almohad dominance of Spain ended with defeat in 1212 at the Battle of Las Navas de Tolosa while, in Africa, they lost their territories gradually. The last Almohad caliph, Idris II (ruled 1266–1269), was murdered by a slave. The Marinid dynasty replaced the Almohads, ruling Morocco for the next two hundred years.

Meanwhile, following the conquest of Egypt in 639, Sunni Islam had been introduced and, for the next six centuries, Egypt was ruled by nominees of the Islamic Caliphate, firstly from Baghdad and then from Cairo which the Fatimid Dynasty named as its capital. The Shi'a Fatimids were good for Egypt. Irrigation was improved, with dams and canals being repaired and agricultural production increased. It became a successful manufacturer of linen and cotton cloth and its trade with the countries of the Mediterranean and the Red Sea prospered. As ever, however, the heaviest tax burden fell on the peasant farmers – the *fellahin*.

The Crusades, launched in 1095 by Pope Urban II at the Council of Clermont, threatened Fatimid Egypt in the 1160s. A leader emerged, however, in the Kurdish general Salah ad-Din Yusuf ibn Ayyub, known in English as Saladin (ruled 1174–93). In 1171, when the Fatimid ruler of Egypt died, Saladin replaced him, founding the Ayyubid dynasty and returning the country to Sunni Islam. Cairo flourished, becoming a leading centre of Arabic learning and, in 1187, Saladin defeated the crusaders and re-took Jerusalem.

In the fourteenth century, the Black Death arrived. It had first appeared in the Gobi Desert in Mongolia and had rapidly spread across Europe, killing 40 per cent of the population before crossing into North Africa via Spain and Sicily. It did unparalleled damage, killing a third of the population of Egypt and casting the region into a catastrophic decline. Around the same time, the Ayyubid dynasty was overthrown. Under Saladin Mamluk slaves, who had been recruited as soldiers from Turkey and southern Russia, became an influential class in Egypt. Eventually they defeated the ruling Ayyubid dynasty there in 1250, creating the Mamluk dynasty that ruled for the next 250 years. The Mamluks conquered Syria and Palestine, saw off the crusaders and prevented Mongol invaders from overrunning the country in 1260. But, as other armies came to grips with handguns and cannons, the Mamluks failed to do so. Furthermore, the Egyptian infrastructure fell into disrepair and agricultural production declined. In 1517, this negligence resulted in conquest by the Ottoman Turks but the hereditary ruling Mamluks returned to power as *beys*, Pashas or viceroys during the seventeenth and eighteenth centuries. In 1798, when French general Napoleon Bonaparte's (ruled 1799–1815) army invaded Egypt, it met little resistance. It was left to the British and the Ottoman Turks to oust the French in 1801. This would mark the beginning of a century of Anglo-French rivalry over Egypt.

Unlike Africa to the north, East Africa was Islamised gradually by people from the Arab Peninsula, just fifty miles across the sea, as well as from Egypt, Somalia and Persia. They came as traders and, indeed, as in North Africa, trade was an important factor in the spread of Islam. Kanem, near Lake Chad, was converted to Islam in the ninth century while, in Ghana, the kings were not Muslims but Muslims occupied senior positions in their government and lived peaceably amongst the non-Muslim peoples of the empire. The powerful empire of Mali became a seat of Muslim learning. By the fourteenth century, the rulers of the Hausa city states – Gobir, Katsina, Kano, Zazzau, Zamfara and Kebbi – were all Muslim. Only when the Fulbe launched their *jihads* in the eighteenth century did the majority of the people of these states convert. By the 1880s, Islam was the religion of a third of the African continent.

Trade

The Camel

Crossing the Sahara entailed a perilous journey of fifteen hundred miles, across treacherous terrain, in the face of both human and animal predators as well as deadly sandstorms. Food sources were non-existent and oases were far apart. Nonetheless, Arabs and Africans alike craved each other's goods and huge caravans of camels established routes across the sands in order to satisfy these needs. It would not have been possible without the dromedary camel's astonishing capacity to carry a load of about a hundred and thirty kilos between thirty and sixty miles a day. Crucially, the camel could do this for ten days without fresh water, and was able to withstand the extreme heat of the day as well as the piercing chill of the desert night. By the fourth century, the camel had replaced the pack-ox as the main beast of burden across the Maghreb, helping the Berbers to establish the important long-distance trans-Saharan trading network. Regular caravans were organised by Sanhaja Berbers and Tuareg cameleers who were led by Toubou guides along tracks first used around 500 BC. By the twelfth century, caravans of 12,000 camels were being recorded.

Slaves were a constant feature of the trade but other goods such as gold, ivory and kola nuts – containing the mild stimulant caffeine – were also carried. Before the discovery of the New World in the sixteenth century, all the gold used in Europe was mined in West Africa and transported along these routes, bringing extraordinary wealth to the rulers of the western Sudanic kingdoms. The gold was used by the West Africans to obtain salt, which was important because there are few sources of salt south of the Sahara. The demand was, consequently, enormous.

Empires and Trade

There have been numerous small Sudanic states in the last fifteen hundred years, several of which are remembered as 'empires', most notably Ghana which lasted from around 700 to 1240, Mali (c. 1235–c. 1599), Kanem-Bornu (c. 1068–1846) and the Songhai (1464–1591).

Dominating the southern part of modern Mauritania and Mali between the fifth and thirteenth centuries, the people of Ghana were Soninke who worked as farmers, fishermen and herdsmen. The name 'Ghana' was derived from the name of the empire's ruler, the 'Ghana', and should not be confused with the modern state of the same name which is located eight hundred kilometres to the south-east.

Ghana, a grouping of chiefdoms in the Sahel grassland south of the Sahara, was a product of the larger and more settled communities formed by iron working farmers who had probably used iron age technology to fashion spears and swords. This superior weaponry gave them an advantage over less advanced and poorly organised neighbours. The Soninke also possessed horses, obtained from Saharan nomads. The military benefits provided by these two developments ensured their superiority over their neighbours. However, although they may have been superior to their neighbours, raids by Sanhaja-Berber nomads of the western Sahara could only be defended by grouping together, marking the beginnings of a state. The state's location in the western Sahel – midway between the desert which was the principal source of salt, and the goldfields of the upper Senegal River – allowed the Soninke to act as middlemen in the reciprocal trade of salt and gold, enabling them to grow wealthy and powerful. As the trans-Saharan trade in gold increased in the ninth and tenth centuries, so, too, did the status and power of Ghana.

Ghana's decline started at the end of the twelfth century, by which time it had lost its domination of the western Sudan gold trade. Sometime after 1050, it had converted to Islam which coincided with the opening up of new goldfields at Bure to the south and trans-Saharan trade routes being opened up to the east. Both events allowed the peoples of those areas to become strong enough to assert their independence. In the early thirteenth century, the Southern Soninke chiefdom of Sosso took over most of what had been the Empire of Ghana, also conquering the Malinke to the south. A critical factor in the empire's decline, however, was environmental deterioration. The land could no longer support the increased population, while, at the same time, Berber pastoralists were pushing southwards and overgrazing. In the early thirteenth century, Soninke merchants and traders deserted the Ghanaian capital, Kumbi-Saleh, settling to the south and west and helping to develop trade in other parts of West Africa as well as stimulating the formation of new states.

Across sub-Saharan West Africa, people were also beginning to organise themselves into large and small settlements, the larger ones inevitably forming close to important trade routes. Taxation of this trade made local rulers wealthy and powerful. The empire of Kanem emerged around 900, north-east of Lake Chad. It was ruled by a dynasty known as Sayfawa – at 771 years the longest continuous dynasty in African history. Initially nomadic, at the end of the eleventh century, under the leadership of Humai ibn Salamna (ruled 1068–80), this people created a capital at Njimi and became wealthy through control of trade across the central Sahara. Kanem was at the height of its power during the reign of Mai Dunama Dabbalemi ibn Salma (ruled 1221–1259) but slipped into decline shortly after, following succession disputes and raids by the Tuareg and the Bulala. In the sixteenth century, however, having fled to an area west of Lake Chad in Bornu, the Kanem rulers expanded their territory and re-established their grip on Trans-Saharan trade. They ruled Kanem-Bornu until it was incorporated into the Ouaddai Empire and the last of their leaders died in 1846.

Lasting from around 1230 to 1600, the Mali (or Mandingo) Empire was founded by Sundiata Keita (c. 1217–c. 1255) who conquered lands eastwards to the Niger bend, northwards into the Sahara and west to the Atlantic from his base in present-day northern Guinea and southern Mali. The empire reached its peak in the fourteenth century when its ruler Mansa Musa I (ruled c. 1312–c. 1337) made a legendary pilgrimage to Mecca, accompanied by 60,000 troops, 12,000 slaves and a huge amount of gold that he distributed en route, making a huge impression on the Muslim and European world. After 1599, the empire lost the goldfields that made it rich and disintegrated. It was replaced by the Songhai Empire founded by warrior king Sunni Ali Ber (c. 1464–c. 1492) that stretched across present-day Niger and Burkina Faso, westwards from its capital Gao to the trading centre of Jenne.

Trade Across the Indian Ocean

Trade was carried out between the people of East Africa and southern Arabia by dhows sailing the Sabaean Lane, the passageway named after the southern Arabian Kingdom of Saba. As ever, gold, ivory and slaves made up the bulk of the commodities being sent from Africa, and cloth, porcelain, salt and hardware travelled in the opposite direction. This trade was reliant on the prevailing seasonal climatic and tidal conditions. From November until March, monsoon winds blow from the north-east, assisted by the Equatorial Current that creates a passage along the East African coast. Merchants took advantage of these conditions to bring goods from Asia to Africa. Then, from May until October, the monsoon winds blow in the opposite direction. With the help of the Central Indian Ocean current, these winds took the dhows back to Asia laden with goods from Africa.

There was considerable rivalry amongst the Greek successor states that emerged following the death of Alexander the Great. The Seleucid Empire, which at its peak included central Anatolia, the Levant, Mesopotamia, Persia, today's Turkmenistan, Pamir and parts of Pakistan, exercised strict control over the land routes to India which forced the Ptolemies – the Greek ruling family of Egypt – to find their ivory elsewhere. To this end, they created a string of elephant hunting stations as far as the mouth of the Red Sea, boosting the ivory trade in the region. When Ptolemy V (204–281 BC) lost Syria, the Egyptians were forced to use the southern sea route in order to trade with India. The Greek navigator Eudoxus of Cyzicus, who lived around 130 BC, made the first direct voyage by a Greek to India, leading to an increase in the trade in Oriental luxuries.

The Roman Empire later became a useful market for oriental luxury goods but the Romans sought to break the Arabs' grip on the trade. The Arabs, however, appear to have had a virtual monopoly on trade with the East African coast. The Roman demand for ivory increased and, by the first century after the birth of Christ, it was only available from deep in the African interior, in the region of the Upper Nile, and was supplied from Adulis. As a result, ivory from the East African coast, although believed to be of lower quality, assumed a new importance, bringing East Africa into the international trading system centred on the Mediterranean. This created a melange of peoples making up a class of coastal traders who participated in international trade. This trade foundered, however, when Rome entered its long period of decline in the third century.

Later, in the sixth and seventh centuries, the Persians became the dominant maritime power in the Western Indian Ocean and a commanding commercial presence on the coast of East Africa. The ivory trade had lost its Mediterranean market but, by the tenth century, India's demand began to outstrip its domestic supply, leading it, along with a burgeoning Chinese market, to turn to East Africa.

Swahili

Swahili or Kiswahili is today the most widely spoken of the African languages of eastern Africa, spoken by various ethnic groups inhabiting large stretches of the Indian Ocean coastline from northern Kenya to northern Mozambique. Derived from the Arabic word *sahil*, meaning 'coast', it means literally 'the people of the coast' and is today the official language of Tanzania, Kenya, Uganda and the Democratic Republic of the Congo.

The term 'Swahili' began to be used between the tenth and

fourteenth centuries to describe a coastal society that was a mixture of Islamic and African. The Swahilis traded with the Arabs, Persians, Somalis, Indians, Indonesians and people of the Orient, the wealth this trade produced enabling the development of a distinctive Swahili culture. The main trading towns were Shanga, Pate and Lamu in the north, Mombasa in the central coastal area and Kilwa to the south. In exchange for the customary African exports of ivory, slaves, gold, animal skins and pearls, the Swahilis received luxury goods from around the world.

By the beginning of the thirteenth century, Kilwa had broken the grip on the gold trade long held by the merchants of Mogadishu to the north in modern-day Somalia. Kilwa merchants established a small trading settlement at Sofala, south of modern Beira, and welcomed gold from the emerging societies of the Limpopo valley and the Zimbabwe plateau, making their state perhaps the wealthiest of the Swahili city-states for the next two centuries. The literate classes read Swahili poetry, written in Arabic script, and in the fifteenth and sixteenth centuries an architectural golden age was enjoyed, in which magnificent mosques, palaces, harbours and public baths were built.

Between 1050 and 1200, Muslim immigration from the Persian Gulf and Oman had forced a number of Swahili Muslims to move southwards, settling on the islands of Zanzibar, Mafia, Pemba and the Comoros, establishing new trading centres, building houses made from blocks of coral stone and founding dynasties that would rule for centuries to come. These people became known as Shirazi, due to the origins of their ancestors in Shiraz in the Persian Gulf.

Central and Southern Africa until 1600

Historians describe the period in central and southern Africa after about 1000 as the 'Later Iron Age'. Fundamentally, it was a time of great political, economic and social change. Techniques in agriculture, fishing and manufacture improved but it was on agriculture that the economic status of the state depended. In the south, people learned to exploit the drier grasslands and there was an increase in cattle-rearing. Different communities had different specialities, resulting in cross-fertilisation as regions traded with each other. Stone Age hunter-gatherers disappeared as land was brought into agricultural or pastoral use.

Society shifted from village-based communities to larger political groups, led by territorial chiefs whose power and prestige had increased. Often these chiefdoms attributed their origins to a mythical figure from whom the chiefs were descended. The ruler was more often than not considered to be divine and to constitute a contact with the spiritual world, for there was little distinction between religion and state. The elite class that supported the ruler depended to a large extent on him as he did on them, and he distributed land and labour accordingly.

Just over one hundred and fifty miles from Harare, capital of modern-day Zimbabwe, stand the remains of southern Africa's most famous stone building. Its construction is believed to have taken place over a long period, from 1200 to 1450, its builders thought to have been the Karanga, a branch of the Shona-speaking people who had immigrated to the Zimbabwe plateau from the Kingdom of Mapungubwe in the thirteenth century. The Zimbabwean rulers created an extraordinary culture around their royal palace at Great Zimbabwe. They had complex stone walls and structures built, funded by the approximately 150 tributary states that they controlled, an empire bigger than those of Mapungubwe, Butua or Mutapa. It covered an immense area between the Limpopo and Zambezi rivers, extending into present-day Mozambique and Botswana as well as the Transvaal area of modern South Africa. Wealth also derived from the ivory and gold that was transported to Africa's south-eastern coast from the interior. In return Arabic goods were imported into the kingdom. It is thought that there may have been environmental reasons for Great Zimbabwe's eventual decline – over-grazing and drought. Or that the people of the kingdom had to move to follow trade routes and continue their involvement in the gold trade. By 1450, Great Zimbabwe and much of the remainder of the kingdom had been abandoned.

In west-central Africa, the Kingdom of the Kongo was located in what are now, northern Angola, the Republic of the Congo and the western part of the Democratic Republic of the Congo. It originated in small Iron Age communities that lived north of the Malebo Pool and amalgamated into a federation under their ruler, the Manikongo, by the fifteenth century. The monarchy would last until 1914 when it was dissolved by the Portuguese. Prosperity brought a growing population that put pressure on food supplies, leading the Manikongo to send out expeditions to establish outposts and extend the kingdom's borders. Stretching from the Atlantic in the west, to the Kwango River in the east, and with a population of more than half a million, and a land area of almost 50,000 square miles, at its height it was the largest state in western central Africa.

The Arrival of the Europeans and the Beginning of the Slave Trade

The Portuguese and the East African Coast

By the fifteenth century, although North Africa and the coasts of the Red Sea and East Africa were well charted, knowledge of Africa south of the Sahara was scant. In their ignorance, Europeans believed those territories to be peopled by exotic and fierce people known as 'Ethiopians', a term that had nothing to do with the real Ethiopians who lived in north-East Africa. It was the desire to expand this knowledge and to discover a means of controlling the fantastically lucrative trade in spice, slaves and gold that drove Portugal's Prince Henry 'the Navigator' (1394–1460) to encourage voyages of exploration by Portuguese vessels along the West African coast. The wealth of the east was needed to help defend the country against its powerful neighbour, Spain, but there was the added benefit of converting the peoples of West Africa to Christianity, and recruiting them to fight the relentless tide of Islam. A new type of ship, the round-bottomed caravel, allowed Portuguese sailors to negotiate the West African coast, and the first visit took place in 1422 when two captains brought back gold, salt and ten slaves, the first of many such cargos.

The Portuguese reached the Akan goldfields in modern day Ghana in the 1470s, constructing a fort at Elmina ('the mine'). Soon, half the gold from the Akan goldfields was being diverted to the European trading posts on the coast, away from the trans-Saharan trade, and shipped northwards. This wealth funded the further exploration of the African coast and the eventual circumnavigation of Africa that finally provided a sea route to India. In 1488, Bartolomeu Dias (c.

1451–1500) rounded the Cape of Good Hope, sailing as far as Mossel Bay, east of the Cape, where his crew refused to travel any further. He returned to Portugal but had proved that Africa could be circumnavigated. In 1498, Portuguese explorer Vasco da Gama (c. 1460–1524) and four caravels rounded the Cape of Good Hope and sailed northwards along the coast of East Africa, the first Europeans to enter the Indian Ocean from the south. Astonished by the wealth in produce, cloth and gold of the Swahili coastal city-states, they plundered Mozambique, looted Arab trading ships, fought off the Swahilis at Mombasa and eventually sailed onward to Calicut in India where they arrived on May 20. Only two of da Gama's ships made it back to Portugal where they arrived in July and August 1499.

Numerous expeditions followed. In the name of a 'holy Christian war' against Islam, they sailed their heavily armed ships into harbours, demanding that rulers become Portuguese subjects and pay a hefty tribute to the Portuguese king. If this condition was not met, the town was attacked, possessions seized and reluctant Muslims were put to death. By the end of the first decade of the sixteenth century, the Portuguese had established fortresses in the southern ports of Kilwa, Sofala and Mozambique, ensuring not only a base from which to set sail to their Indian colony of Goa, but also from which to control the gold that came from the Zimbabwe Plateau. Eventually, to pacify the rebellious city of Mombasa, the Portuguese built the massive Fort Jesus there which became their administrative capital for the next century. Its massive stone walls symbolised the violence with which Portugal would exercise its authority over commerce along the East African coastline during the sixteenth and seventeenth centuries.

The Impact of the Old World on Africa

The arrival of Europeans inevitably brought great change to Africa. One of the least desirable elements of that change, however, was disease. Africa, of course, already had its own diseases, amongst them sleeping sickness, bilharzia and malaria. The arrival of the Portuguese, English, French and other Europeans brought new killer diseases such as the European strain of smallpox against which Africans had no natural immunity and which claimed countless lives in Africa between the sixteenth and nineteenth centuries. Syphilis, like smallpox, was already present in a mild form, but the more deadly European strain spread rapidly in the sixteenth century. In the following century, typhus and tuberculosis appeared and, at around the same time, the pneumonic plague – the Black Death – which had previously been prevented from reaching sub-Saharan Africa by the desert arrived via the Atlantic slave trade in the Kongo and Angola. By the eighteenth century, it had struck Senegal and Guinea. All of these diseases prevented the population of the continent from growing in the same way as it did in more temperate climes.

It was not all bad news, however. The Europeans also introduced highly productive crops from the New World, such as maize which replaced sorghum, and cassava which became the preferred African tuber food. They also introduced a wide variety of beans – including kidney, lima and navy – as well as the sweet potato from Central America; the potato, which arrived from America, via England, in the eighteenth century; peanuts, which were introduced in the sixteenth century and flourished; and peas, sugar cane and sesame from Asia.

The greatest and most enduring consequence of the arrival of Europeans in Africa, however, was the slave trade. For centuries, it would devastate the continent, stripping it of its productive young men and women, destroying its social structures and erasing its traditions and cultures.

The Slave Trade

'To overdraw its evils is a simple impossibility… We passed a slave woman shot or stabbed through the body and lying on the path. [Onlookers] said an Arab who passed early that morning had done it in anger at losing the price he had given for her, because she was unable to walk any longer. We passed a woman tied by the neck to a tree and dead… We came upon a man dead from starvation… The strangest disease I have seen in this country seems really to be broken heartedness, and it attacks free men who have been captured and made slaves.'

Explorer and missionary, David Livingstone,
on the slave trade

The oldest evidence of slavery in Africa dates back to 2,900 BC, in carvings and inscriptions found at the second cataract on the Nile. Various organisations and non-governmental agencies report that it continues in Africa to this day, in countries such as Mauritania, Niger and the Sudan. In three kingdoms – Loango, Tio and Kongo – that emerged north and south of the Congo River before the arrival of the Portuguese, captives taken in war or in raids were used as slaves by both the aristocracy and commoners. The army of the ruler of the Kongo consisted of around 20,000 slave soldiers. On the arrival of the Portuguese, however, slaves became the principal item of trade.

In the 1480s, Portuguese settlers used slave labour in the sugar plantations on the islands of São Tomé and Príncipé off the African coast in the Gulf of Guinea. Slaves had already been used in the cultivation of sugar cane on islands in the Mediterranean and in southern Spain and Portugal. It was not only North Africa that provided these slaves but also the Slavs of southern Russia, from whom the name 'slave' derives. São Tomé became the largest supplier of sugar, for which Europeans had an insatiable hunger, and its plantation system, using African slave labour, provided the template for plantation development in the New World.

In the beginning, in the fifteenth and early sixteenth centuries, slaves were taken mainly from the regions of modern Senegal and Gambia to be used in plantations and farms in southern Spain and Portugal. While the Portuguese had been opening up the sea route around the Cape to India, however, their Spanish neighbours had been forging a trans-Atlantic route to the Americas and the Caribbean. Labour was in demand, to work in gold and silver mines as well as in tobacco plantations, but the local population had been decimated both by the harsh treatment of their new masters and by the diseases that had been unwittingly introduced from Europe. For instance, ninety per cent of the Amerindian population of the Caribbean islands was wiped out after a century of European presence. The colonisers imported criminals and undesirables from Europe, but there were not enough for the work that needed to be done. They quickly decided that Africans were the solution.

The first batch of slaves left Africa in 1532 but, for the first hundred years, the numbers were relatively insignificant. From 1630, however, with the added involvement of the Dutch, the French and the English and a growth in the number of sugar plantations in Brazil and the Caribbean, the number of slaves being shipped from Africa to the Americas rapidly escalated. The next two centuries witnessed the greatest forced relocation of captive people in history. In the seventeenth century, the number of transported slaves increased to around 20,000 a year. In the eighteenth century, somewhere between 50,000 and 100,000 Africans were transported across the Atlantic each year. It is estimated that a total of around 10 million Africans disembarked in the Americas alive while at least a further 2 million died during the voyage. Some historians argue that the correct number is possibly double that.

The western coast of Nigeria became known as 'the slave coast' but, during the eighteenth century, virtually every part of Africa's Atlantic coastline was involved in the trade. It moved down from its origins in Senegambia to Upper Guinea and the Windward Coast, to the Gold Coast, the Bights of Benin and Biafra and finally west-central Africa from which the greatest number of slaves was taken – 2,331,800. The slaves came, on the whole, from the interior, but Europeans rarely ventured there in search of them. On the rare occasion that they did, they were usually defeated by the local people or disease. They restricted their activities, therefore, to their trading forts on the coast, for which they paid tribute to local chiefs who grew wealthy from the supply of captives – mostly taken in war and rarely from their own society, unless they were criminals or outcasts. African and European slave-dealers were then responsible for conveying them to the coast for sale and transportation.

The wars were often campaigns involving the creation of states or the expansion of existing ones. Wars waged by Benin in the late fifteenth century, the Muslim Fulbe of Futa Jalon in modern Guinea in the early eighteenth century and by the growing states of Oyo, Dahomey and Ashanti in the seventeenth and eighteenth centuries, produced large numbers of slaves. Although wars were never fought purely to create slaves, the high prices on offer for them at the coast undoubtedly encouraged military conflict. When guns were offered in exchange for captives in the eighteenth century, there was even greater incentive to go to war.

The loss to Africa was, of course, immense. Not only did slavery seriously damage the economic wellbeing of the region; it also destroyed traditional cultures and introduced a disregard for the value of human life. People were quite simply regarded as property. Crucially, it resulted in huge numbers of productive young people – mostly men, aged between 14 and 35 – leaving Africa, their productivity lost to their continent forever. The cruelty was unimaginable. Sold by local chiefs to slave-dealers, slaves were chained up and marched to the coast where they were locked up in cages. When the next European slave ship arrived, they were stripped naked, regardless of gender, and examined to ensure that they were sufficiently fit and healthy to be purchased. Once sold to a European slave merchant, they were herded onto a ship and made to lie on decks which were arranged like shelves. It was impossible to sit up straight, let alone stand and they lay in their own urine and excreta for weeks on end. The slaves, many of whom believed that the crew were cannibals, were terrified of the vast ocean. During the thirty days of the crossing, supplies of food and drink were limited and of poor quality. During the sixteenth century, 20 per cent of slaves failed to survive the voyage and captains allowed for this by cramming in even more. With improved food, by the nineteenth century this was reduced to 10 per cent. Life was still short, however, and, in the time remaining to them, slaves endured appalling degradation and suffering.

Once at their destination, the hardship did not end, of course. They were worked hard and badly malnourished. A third of slaves died after three years and very few survived more than ten. But fresh bodies were being brought in all the time, because it proved cheaper to import a new batch of slaves than to rely on slaves bringing up their own children. After all, a woman could not work effectively if she was pregnant and a child would be unable to work for the first few years of its life.

Of course, for the European merchants, there were vast profits to be made, and not just from slaves. They constituted only one part of a lucrative triangular trade. At each stage of the triangle, the merchant made a profit. Firstly, he would send European goods to Africa which were exchanged for slaves. The slaves were sent to the Americas and cash crops were sent back to Europe. Needless to say, the dependence on imported European manufactured goods led to a decline in traditional African craft industries. Once across the ocean, slaves were sold for around two or three times what they had cost on the African coast or were bartered for sugar to be shipped to Europe. Profits were huge and a number of cities such as Bristol, Liverpool, Nantes, Bordeaux and Amsterdam grew wealthy on them. The money that was made in the English ports contributed significantly to the funding of the industrial revolution in Britain.

Other Slave Routes

It is unknown how many slaves were sent from Africa to the countries bordering the Mediterranean, the Middle East and the Indian Ocean before the arrival of the Arabs in the seventh century. It is estimated, however, that between 800 and 1900, more than 12 million slaves were transported to Asia, a number approximating that of the Transatlantic slave trade. (However, the latter occurred over a period of only 400 years; the figure for the Asian slave trade was arrived at over eleven centuries.) Muslim merchants established complex networks for transporting slaves across the Sahara, the Red Sea and the Indian Ocean. The eventual Muslim master had the responsibility to ensure the conversion to Islam of non-Muslim slaves and, for the slaves, conversion was necessary in order to obtain freedom.

Conversion also allowed slaves to do more complex work than just agricultural labouring. Slave bureaucrats and soldiers were needed to run and defend the huge Arab empire. Sometimes they even wielded authority over free citizens of the state.

For many centuries, slaves were conveyed on a regular basis across the Sahara. Between 5,000 and 10,000, supplied to Muslim merchants by the rulers of the Sudanic states, are estimated to have been transported every year until the fifteenth century. In each of the seventeenth and eighteenth centuries, the six northward routes across the Sahara carried around 700,000 slaves. This represented a massive increase in numbers, around 67 per cent of the total number of slaves who had been transported in 800 years.

In the nineteenth century, as the Trans-Saharan slave trade declined, there was an increase in the Nilotic trade. In 1820, Egyptian leader Muhammad Ali (ruled 1805–48) sent his army into Sudan in search of slaves for his army. Meanwhile, the Egyptian governor-general sent expeditions along the Blue and White Niles. By 1838, around 10,000 slaves were being marched down the Nile and across the Nubian Desert every year.

Even older than the Trans-Saharan slave trade was the trafficking in slaves across the Red Sea. The Ancient Egyptians regularly sent trading expeditions to the Land of Punt – believed to have been located in the Arabian Peninsula – northern Somalia and the Red Sea coasts which returned with slaves as well as other goods. There is also little doubt that slaves would have been transported across the Red Sea from Africa to Arabia during Greek and Roman rule in Egypt. Later, the trade probably accounted for a modest 2,000 slaves a year and, by the seventeenth century, this number is estimated to have come down to around 1,000 slaves a year. It rose again to 2,000 in the following century, mostly sourced from Ethiopia and the Nile Valley.

Slaves were also exported to Asia, although the numbers are unclear. However, around 80,000 slaves were marched to the coast from the African interior by 1810, some remaining on the coast while most were conveyed to Arabia, Persia and India, as well as to the Americas, the most common destination. In 1873, the Sultan of

Zanzibar, Barghash bin Said Al-Busaid (ruled 1870–1888), was persuaded by the British government – with the compelling support of the Royal Navy – to enact a ban on all trade of slaves by sea.

The End of the Atlantic Slave Trade

As the eighteenth century progressed, Britain became the largest exporter of Africans, more than half of all those captured ending up on British ships crossing the Atlantic. But moves were already afoot to bring an end to this shameful trade. In 1792, Denmark became the first European country to ban the trade with legislation that took effect in 1803. In 1807, the British made it illegal for British subjects to transport slaves across the Atlantic for the purpose of selling them into slavery. In 1808, the United States banned the importation of slaves; Holland banned the slave trade in 1814 and France followed suit in 1817.

The abolition, however, was not entirely on humanitarian grounds. In fact, by the beginning of the nineteenth century, the slave trade was no longer as lucrative as it had once been. The price of sugar had fallen as a result of over-production in the Caribbean and the French were producing cheaper sugar. Furthermore, slave prices had escalated and profits were falling. Investment by European bankers moved away from the plantations in the Americas back to manufacturing at home as a result of the Industrial Revolution. Meanwhile, capitalist factory owners realised that 'free' workers would spend their wages on goods made in their factories and Africa could become a lucrative market for their goods. Leaving Africans in Africa would provide such a market. In return, raw materials could be obtained from Africa. The European perception of the continent was changing.

Africans had themselves struggled to bring an end to the trade. In England two former slaves from West Africa – Ottobah Cugoano (c. 1757–after 1791) and Olaudah Equiano (c. 1745–97) campaigned for abolition in books published in the late 1780s. Equiano's autobiography became a bestseller. And, of course, Africans had always resisted being captured and sold as slaves, staging revolts on ships as well as after their arrival at their destination. In Brazil in the seventeenth century, escaped slaves established an independent republic known as Palmares that lasted from 1605 until 1694 when it was suppressed. The most dramatic slave revolt, led by a slave known by the French name of Toussaint L'Ouverture, occurred in the French colony of St. Dominique – modern-day Haiti – in 1791. The rebels declared the Republic of Haiti in 1804 and their action had a huge impact on European governments' attitudes to the slave trade.

Following the British government's criminalisation of the slave trade, it was anxious to start profiting from trade with Africa and took steps to encourage other nations either to stop or reduce their involvement. Britain established an 'Anti-Slavery Squadron' which patrolled the seas off West Africa. Nevertheless, the plantations in the Americas continued to receive a supply of slaves, 1.3 million being transported across the Atlantic between 1807 and 1888. The final abolition of all aspects of slavery in British colonies came in 1834, in French colonies in 1848, in Cuba in 1860, in the southern United States in 1865 and in Brazil in 1888.

The Legitimisation of Trade in Africa

The slave trade had torn apart the West African coast and interior for centuries. Agricultural production had been decimated by war and society was divided between the ruling and trading elite and the peasantry. There were some positives, nonetheless. For a start, African farmers had embraced the new crops from the Americas. And trade between peoples of the interior had continued as well as trade with the Europeans on the coast. The commodities that replaced slaves included gum Arabic, groundnuts, and palm oil which was the principal lubricant for Europe's industrial machinery prior to the introduction of petroleum oil. It became West Africa's most important export. Inevitably, such a lucrative trade led to conflict, especially as Europeans sought to deal directly with producers. During the second half of the nineteenth century, however, the British gradually gained control of the palm oil trade in the Niger delta.

Slaves continued to be traded, especially from states like Dahomey, while the civil wars in the Oyo Empire in the 1830s and 1840s ensured a ready supply. It was only with the closure of the slave markets in Cuba and the United States that the trade really slowed down. In general terms, however, little changed. The rulers and merchants increased their wealth while the remainder of the population's circumstances were little altered or grew even worse. European imports, of course, inhibited the growth of indigenous industries. African rulers were able to purchase more modern firearms, but they were never allowed to get their hands on the type of modern weaponry that the Europeans used against them. Even Africa's internal trade fell victim to foreign interference as European traders sought to control it, cutting out African middlemen. This would lead eventually to the so-called 'Scramble for Africa' towards the end of the nineteenth century.

Liberia and Sierra Leone

The settlement of Granville Town was established in Sierra Leone in 1787 when four hundred freed slaves arrived off the coast, accompanied by some English traders, their journey organised by British abolitionists. In the 1790s, more freed slaves arrived from Nova Scotia in Canada and, in 1808, as thousands of slaves arrived, freed following the 1807 abolition, Britain claimed the settlement as a colony. The British Anti-Slavery Squadron brought slaves freed from captured slaving ships and the nineteenth century saw the arrival of many former slaves from America. Christian missionaries arrived in the area bringing not only religion but European-style education as well. Indeed, many Christians from Sierra Leone travelled widely in West Africa as missionaries.

Liberia, Sierra Leone's southern neighbour, was established in 1820 when the American Colonization Society started to send black volunteers to the area known as the Pepper Coast, south of Sierra Leone, with the objective of establishing a colony for freed slaves.

Their intentions were not entirely charitable – they believed that the presence of freed slaves in America's southern states would destabilise those who remained in slavery. Neither were their methods of acquiring land sensitive to the peoples who had been living there for centuries, much of it being purchased at gunpoint.

Educated blacks increasingly replaced the American whites who had been administrating the territory and, in 1847, the Republic of Liberia was proclaimed, the name deriving from the Latin word *liber*, meaning 'free'. Its capital was called Monrovia, after US President James Monroe, and its constitution was based on that of the United States. The indigenous people were gradually integrated into the cultural, social and political life of the country. Sierra Leone eventually became a British colony, but Liberia maintained its precarious independence even during the 'scramble for Africa' towards the end of the century.

Sub-Saharan Africa
to the Eighteenth Century

West Africa

Created by the fifty to eighty inches of rain that falls on it every year, a dense, 200 mile-wide tract of tropical rainforest stretches from the Senegambia in the west to Cameroon in the east. Its sheer impenetrability meant that it took a long time to settle and cultivate it but, by 1,000 BC, villages with earthen fortifications had been established and areas of the forest had been cleared using iron tools. The new crop, the yam, was cultivated and supplemented in the diet by fish. Communities were highly organised, a necessity in equatorial agriculture. Soon, the inhabited compounds had begun to evolve into states, each of which developed in its own way, with its own character and culture.

From the early fifteenth to the late sixteenth century, Songhai was one of the largest Islamic empires in history. It began to go into decline, however, during the sixteenth century, weakened by a series of short reigns and internecine disputes that resulted in civil war in the 1580s. Drought and disease exacerbated the situation while, as trans-Saharan trade was drawn away to the east, the Songhai lost control of their long-distance trading routes. Meanwhile, the gold miners of the Akan forest began to trade directly with the Europeans who had begun to establish themselves on the coast.

As the sixteenth century drew to a close, the Songhai rulers nonetheless seemed unconcerned. Their people were contented; they had not been unduly oppressed or had to deal with high taxation to fund military adventures or to defend their empire. In fact, their country had not faced a military threat for a century and rulers had, consequently, not felt the need to modernise their army by importing the primitive, unreliable firearms that some states had felt necessary.

In the opening months of 1591, the Moroccans invaded Songhai. The Songhai had trusted the Sahara desert to provide an adequate bulwark but the lure of the trans-Saharan gold trade proved too seductive for the Moroccan sultan Ahmad al-Mansur (ruled 1578–1603). His small elite force of around 4,000 men, armed with the latest muzzle-loading weapons, defeated the Songhai at the Battle of Tondibi, near Gao. Having lost Timbuktu and Jenne to the Moroccans, Askiya Nuhu (1591–1598), the Songhai ruler, fought a desperate guerrilla campaign. On the death of Sultan Ahmad in 1603, however, the Moroccans lost interest in their sub-Saharan empire. The erstwhile Songhai Empire began to break up, and the individual states that emerged proved independent of Moroccan control. By the middle of the seventeenth century, the Moroccans who stayed behind had ceased paying tribute to their homeland. They ruled the Niger bend – the northern part of the Niger River – until 1737 when Timbuktu was captured by the neighbouring Tuareg who took control of the region.

The Hausa came from a background of nomads from the southern Sahara and the indigenous peoples of the northern Nigerian savannah. They lived in walled villages, their stockades encompassing not just their dwellings, but also large tracts of cultivated land, guaranteed to see them through lengthy sieges. Inevitably, villages began to group together and walled cities began to appear that became the capitals of states whose economies were based on agriculture, trade and manufacturing. These city-states flourished from the sixteenth until the eighteenth century although they cannot be considered to have constituted an empire. They were rivals but no single city succeeded in dominating the others.

Each of these states had its own speciality. One of the most powerful was Gobir, situated in the most northerly part of the region, its pre-eminence coming from trans-Saharan trading links with the eastern edges of the Mali and Songhai empires. Katsina was an important centre for trade and Kano was known for its craftsmen, particularly those who wove cotton cloth, and later for its cloth-dying and leatherwork. Zamfara and Kebbi were also important, while the most southerly, Zazzau, acted as a supplier of slaves to the others. Slaves played an important role in Hausa life, used to construct their city walls and to labour in their fields. In the fourteenth century, the Hausa ruling class embraced Islam, although it was not adopted by their citizens until the eighteenth century. At that point, the corruption of Hausa rulers was denounced by Islamic religious leaders and revolution swept them away in the early nineteenth century.

Yoruba is the Hausa name for the people of the Oyo Empire of western and northern Nigeria. Established in the fourteenth century by the Yoruba, the Oyo Empire became the most politically important state in the region from the mid-seventeenth to the late eighteenth century, also holding power in other kingdoms in what are now Nigeria, Benin and Togo as well as elsewhere. It was responsible for introducing the concept of the large town or city to West Africa. The Yoruba ruler – the *oni* – based his leadership entitlement on direct descent from his people's founding ancestor, the god Oduduwa, lowered to earth in the original Yoruba city-state, Ife, by the god of the sky Olorun.

The model for the Yoruba economy was similar to that of many other states. The fertile soil and high rainfall of Ife enabled them to produce a food surplus that permitted them to feed not just the unproductive ruling elite but also many craftsmen and artists appointed to the court. Meanwhile, the common people who produced this surplus were also subject to taxation. The inhabitants of Oyo relied for their independence on their well-trained cavalry; the region was free of the dreaded tsetse fly as well as many of the other disease-carrying insects to be found in the forest, enabling horses to be used.

Oyo wealth derived partly from its position at the confluence of the long-distance trade routes that carried goods from the rainforest to markets in the Hausa territories to the north and to the busy markets at Gao, Timbuktu and Jenne. It enabled them to expand their territory and, by the eighteenth century, they had conquered kingdoms from the Volta in the west to the Niger in the east. They established a trading relationship with the Europeans at the coast, becoming a major centre for the slave trade and the rewards were reaped by the *alaafin* (ruler) of the time Abiodun (ruled c. 1770–89). He used his wealth to secure control of around 7,000 towns and villages from whom tribute was paid. The empire went into decline, however, as local rulers began to purchase weapons and to distance themselves from the central authority of the *alaafin*. By the 1820s, Oyo had been reduced to a minor state.

Another city-state was developed by the Edo-speaking villagers of the area southwest of Ife. In the eleventh century, these people built the city-state of Benin, its origins lying in rainforest settlements whose inhabitants were clearing the forest using iron tools as early as the fifth century. In the fifteenth century, Benin enjoyed its greatest epoch under the leadership of Ewuare (ruled 1440–73), who created an empire that stretched from the Niger delta in the east to Lagos in the west, and that became one of Africa's pre-eminent powers during the fifteenth and sixteenth centuries. He traded with the Portuguese on the coast, selling them slaves captured in battle and bringing in additional revenue that enabled him, amongst other things, to arm his troops with new weapons such as the crossbow. With the end of Benin's expansion in the early 1500s, however, the sale of slaves stopped. Not until the eighteenth century, when Benin was mired in civil war, did it once again begin exporting slaves. This time, however, it was selling its own citizens. The state went into gradual decline from the middle of the eighteenth century.

In 1650, Dahomey emerged as a power in the region, under the leadership of its king, Houegbadja (ruled 1645–85). A group of Aja people from the coastal region of Allada had settled among the Fon who lived north of Allada. A new kingdom was born in the early seventeenth century. Houegbadja stamped his authority on Dahomey and, as was the case elsewhere, the captives won in his territorial expansion were traded at the coast for firearms, enabling the state to conquer the coastal regions of Allada and Whydah in modern-day Benin. There was constant rivalry between Dahomey and Oyo over slaves and, weakening under the attacks by the fearsome Oyo cavalry, the ruler at the time Agadja (ruled 1708–1740) agreed in 1730 to pay tribute. Nonetheless, Dahomey's expansion continued in the eighteenth century and the king continued to benefit not just from his own slave-trading and taxation of his subjects but from the duties he levied on other Dahomey slave-dealers.

The Ashanti originally lived on the coast of present-day Ghana but moved in the seventeenth century into the interior, north of Lake Bosumtwi where they cleared areas of rainforest between the Pra and Ofin rivers for cultivation and to build villages and towns. In effect, they were initially no more than a group of settlements that, in times of trouble, banded together. It was the legendary leader, Osei Tutu (ruled 1701–17), from the small Kingdom of Kumasi, who founded the Ashanti Confederacy. Having led an alliance of Ashanti states that defeated the dominant Denkyira nation, he persuaded the other leaders to pledge allegiance to him and was crowned *Ashantihene* (king of all the Ashanti).

Osei Tutu united the Ashanti, emphasising their responsibility to the state, and focusing on military service. With training and new fighting techniques and strategies, he transformed his army into a magnificent fighting machine. The defeat of Denkyira had opened a gateway to the coast for the Ashanti and the subsequent trade brought them firearms in exchange for slaves and gold. Using these, the empire was further expanded. Furthermore, to enable swift communication of decisions and orders and to maintain the empire, an extensive road network was constructed. This also proved invaluable in transporting goods for trade from the towns of the interior to the European trading posts on the coast.

Osei Tutu was shot dead by snipers in 1717 while fighting the Akyem in the eastern part of modern-day Ghana and was succeeded by rulers who expanded Ashanti borders to incorporate all of present-day Ghana as well as a great deal of present-day Ivory Coast and Togo. For over a hundred years the Ashanti were the dominant power in the

West African forest, a dominance ended only by the arrival of the British in the nineteenth century.

Central and East Africa

The people of the Zaire forest lived, more often than not, in villages of anything from thirty to two hundred adults, usually related to one another. Brides were exchanged between villages, women were the principal cultivators and slaves were used. People were farmers, fishermen or hunters, sometimes all three, but the pygmies living deep in the forest were specialist hunters, often providing farming communities with meat in exchange for their produce. The staple crops were bananas in the forest and, on the cleared savannah, millet and sorghum. As elsewhere, in the seventeenth and eighteenth centuries, these were replaced by the imported crops of maize and cassava. Trade was carried out using the river network, ending up at the Malebo Pool, in the area of Brazzaville, capital of the modern Republic of the Congo, and, on the opposite bank of the Congo river, Kinshasa, capital of the modern Democratic Republic of the Congo. The area developed into a major trading centre. Shared language, marriage alliances and religious cults linked some of the villages but there were very few large states. Exceptions were the Kuba whose state was bordered by the Sankuru, Lulua, and Kasai rivers; the kingdom of Loango (or Lwaagu) on the coast, its territory stretching from Mayombe in the north almost to the mouth of the Congo River; and the Tio who lived just north of the Malebo Pool in the vicinity of the modern city of Lagos. These were important kingdoms in the transportation of slaves to the coast.

The east-central African savannah saw the Bantu diaspora in the centuries before 1400 by which time they had been assimilated into local communities. The Luba people of the upper Kasai River valley introduced new forms of government that were copied and improved upon by their neighbours, the Lunda. These new ideas then spread across the region. The earliest evidence of the Luba was found at

Sanga on the shores of Lake Kisale, an area that provided ample benefits – rivers and streams were filled with fish and provided a transport infrastructure. The economy was based on fishing, agriculture, mining and hunting.

The Lunda Empire arose in the seventeenth century when a legendary Luba hero Tshibinda Ilunga (c. 1600–1630) married the Lunda Queen Lueji Naweej. He took the title Mwata Yamvo (Lord of the Vipers) and became powerful through the collection of tributes and their re-distribution. The Mwata Yamvo rewarded loyal chiefs with these goods and also used them in commerce, helping to stimulate long-distance trade. Ivory and slaves were traded with Europeans in exchange for guns and woollen cloth, the guns helping the Mwata Yamvo to control trade and to exact tribute. Each Mwata Yamvo was believed to be the living incarnation of his predecessor, meaning that all family ties were cut, dispensing with succession disputes and ensuring continuity.

Trading networks that extended as far as the West African coast brought the new crops from the Americas to the interior. The resulting food surpluses brought stability to the region, a growing population and the cultivation of more land. Lunda tribute collectors created chiefdoms around the edge of the Lunda kingdom, extorting tribute from local farmers and landowners to be sent back to the centre. The most important of these new chiefdoms was the one founded and led by the ruler known as Kazembe (ruled 1740–45). He had been sent by the Mwata Yamvo of the time to capture the salt pans of the upper Lualaba. Lunda influence and tribute collection were extended further east into the copper-producing regions of modern-day Zambia and Zaire and Kazembe II (ruled 1745–60) extended this even further to the east. He established a Lunda state in the valley of the lower Luapula which evolved into an independent empire, grown wealthy on rich, natural resources and control of long-distance trade. By 1800, Kazembe III (ruled 1770s–1804/5) was in control of a vast trans-African trading network, exporting iron, salt, copper, ivory and slaves. Imports included, as ever, guns and woollen goods, as well as cotton cloth from India, glass beads and luxury items for the Kazembe and his court.

The Lozi who lived to the south in the western Zambesi valley faced interesting challenges in the floodplain agriculture they practised. Almost the entire plain was flooded every year, leading the Lozi to build mounds on which they located their villages. When the waters receded, they would plant in the rich, fertile soil left behind. There were areas of the plain that were free of the dreaded tsetse fly, allowing them to herd cattle and they also dammed rivers in order to catch fish. By the end of the seventeenth century, a leader had emerged, known as the Litunga (Keeper of the Earth) who was brought tribute by raiding warriors.

Three dynasties ruled the area that is now southern Malawi. The Kalonga were the most powerful, ruling the Chinyanja-speaking people who lived at the southern end of Lake Malawi. South of them were the Manganja who were ruled by the Lunda dynasty and to the west were the Chewa who were governed by the Undi dynasty. Like the Lunda Empire, they were basically a confederation of chiefdoms which retained ownership of their lands but paid tribute – mainly in the form of food – to the centre.

When, in the late sixteenth century, the Portuguese made an attempt to seize control of the ivory trade in the Zambesi valley, war broke out, and the Shire Valley Lundu army – known as the wa-Zimba – launched ferocious attacks on Portuguese trading settlements. In the early seventeenth century, however, Kalonga Masula (ruled c. 1600–1650) restored peaceful relations with the Portuguese, resuming the trade in ivory. He established a powerful Maravi empire that extended from Mozambique Island in the east to the Zambesi in the west. Following Masula's death, however, it soon became evident that his empire had been entirely dependent on his personal authority, and chiefdoms seized the opportunity to assert their independence.

Another great power in the region in the eighteenth century was the Rozwi Empire which grew out of the Mutapa state, a Shona kingdom stretching from the Zambezi river to the Limpopo river in present-day Zimbabwe and Mozambique. In the first half of the fifteenth century, the Zimbabwe prince sent a party to locate new sources of salt to the north, during which expedition the local people were subjugated. A capital was founded 350 kilometres north of Great Zimbabwe at Zvongombe and, within a generation, the Mutapa state had replaced Great Zimbabwe as the biggest economic and political power in southern Africa. The ruler Matope (ruled c. 1450–80) created an empire that stretched as far as the Indian Ocean, growing rich from copper and ivory. By the time the Portuguese arrived, the empire was the most important and powerful of the region's Shona states.

In 1561, the ruling *mutapa* was converted to Christianity but Muslim merchants based in the capital persuaded the king to murder the priest who had converted him. The Portuguese then used the killing as a pretext for an expedition into the interior in 1568 to seize control of the gold mines and the trade routes on which ivory was exported. As often happened, however, the force was struck down by disease and the remnants limped back to base in 1572. The *mutapa*, meanwhile, levied a fifty per cent tax on all imported goods. The *mutapa* of the time was overthrown in 1629 after trying to expel the Portuguese. The colonists placed their own ruler on the throne and the Mutapa Kingdom became a Portuguese puppet state.

In the seventeenth century, however, a pastoralist people – with origins in the Great Zimbabwe area – created a new regional power in the Butwa kingdom in modern-day south-western Zimbabwe. By the last decade of the century, the leader Changamire (general or king) Dombo (1684–95), at the head of his army the Rozwi, defeated the incumbent *mutapa*. A succession crisis ensued with the Portuguese supporting one candidate and Dombo the other. Soon, however, the latter succeeded in ejecting the Portuguese from their trading posts in Mutapa and neighbouring Manyika and his Rozwi Empire became the pre-eminent state on the Zimbabwe plateau while Mutapa went into decline. The Changamire dynasty remained dominant in the plateau area throughout the eighteenth century, partly due to the ruthless efficiency of the Rozwi army which ensured that tribute payments of food, cattle, skins and ivory were paid. The Portuguese were prohibited from entering the empire.

The East African Interior

The rich, fertile soil and regular rainfall of the agricultural state of Buganda, situated on the northwest shore of Lake Victoria Nyanza, was eminently suited to the cultivation of the banana and the plantain. Within its small area, therefore, the state enjoyed a relatively stable economy as well as a growing population. As with other regions, a centralised government grew out of the need to defend the state against attack by external forces.

Buganda had been founded around the fourteenth century by the Baganda people, whose ancestors had migrated to the region as early as 1000 BC. By the sixteenth century, Buganda was trying to expand its borders but it met with a serious rival in neighbouring Bunyoro, located to the northwest. It may have been partly as a result of raids by Bunyoro that Buganda organised itself into a centralised monarchy, led by a king, known as the *Kabaka*, at the expense of traditional clan chiefs. The local chiefs were rewarded for their loyalty to the *Kabaka* with gifts of land. The country's wealth derived, as ever, from the peasants, through taxes on their harvests. Since banana cultivation was not a labour-intensive task, they were also expected to give their time to public works such as road-building. The roads were good for trade but, as they all passed through the state capital, they provided the *Kabaka* with an effective way of controlling trade in and out of his country. During the eighteenth century, with strong leadership, Buganda became a wealthy and powerful state that dominated the region.

Near Lake Kivu, at the bottom of the western rift, the Kingdom of Rwanda was founded, possibly during the 1600s. In the oral tradition of the country, it is claimed that its founder was *Mwami* Ruganzu (ruled c. 1600–24) who ruled from his capital near Kigali. The elite class was made up of Tutsi pastoralists while the farming class consisted of Hutu people. Although both groups spoke the same Nilotic language, neither was permitted to marry or interact with the other. It took two hundred years for the kingdom to be consolidated under *Mwami* Kigeli IV (1853–95). To the south of Rwanda lay the

Kingdom of Burundi, founded by a Tutsi chief Ntare Rushatsi Cambarantama (ruled 1680–1709) who was said to be Rwandan.

The expansion of the Maasai people was the last stage in the southward migration of Nilotic-speaking pastoralists in the sixteenth or seventeenth century. They dispersed into a number of groupings – the Karamojong and Teso who lived in north-eastern Uganda, the Turkana and Samburu of north-western Kenya and the Maasai who inhabited central Kenya and northern Tanzania. The Maasai had encountered pastoralists who had already occupied the grasslands and seized these lands by force, believing, as they did, that all cattle belonged to them. Age was important to the Maasai as this was the way their society was classified. The three main age groups were children, young adults and elders who were organised in a militaristic way. Boys endured arduous initiation ceremonies and were given military training. As young adults, they were soldiers and herdsmen, both protecting their existing herds and pastures and forming raiding parties to obtain more.

Other peoples existed, such as the Bantu-speaking neighbours of the Maasai, with whom they maintained good relations. There were also fairly large states such as the Chagga, the Pare and the Shambaa in the regions of Kilimanjaro and the Usambara and Pare mountains. The interior was rich in iron and salt which led to the growth of regional trading networks. To the west, the Nyamwezi were important traders. From their base, south of Lake Victoria Nyanza, they forged long-distance trading routes from the kingdoms between the lake and the coast of East Africa.

Southern Africa to the Eighteenth Century

There is plenty of evidence that southern Africa has been settled for a very long time. This is contrary to the claims of some South African whites who long asserted that migrant black Bantu-speaking farmers only crossed the Limpopo into southern Africa at some point in the seventeenth century. Of course, they believed that this notion that South Africa was more or less empty when white settlers arrived there in the seventeenth and eighteenth centuries gave legitimacy to their claims to the land.

In fact, there were a number of societies in southern Africa – Ovambo farmers in the northwest; Herero cattle herders in the north of the modern state of Namibia; groups of Sotho-Tswana origin in the central Highveld east of the Kalahari; Nguni-speakers east of the Drakensberg mountain range, organised into clan-based chiefdoms; Khoisan pastoralists in southern Namibia and in the south-western Cape which they shared with hunter-gatherers; and the Xhosa, also Nguni-speakers, who intermingled with Khoisan cattle- and sheep-herders in the far south, forming new chiefdoms. There was commerce amongst these peoples and with the Portuguese who traded ivory and furs that were distributed across the region's trading network.

The Dutch and English ships that rounded the southern tip of Africa during the sixteenth century used Table Bay, the site of modern-day Cape Town, as a regular stop-off point on the journey, a place where crews could replenish supplies and purchase meat from the local Khoikhoi. The Khoikhoi received iron, copper, tobacco and beads in exchange, but, when supplies became increasingly expensive, the Europeans demanded more animals than the Khoikhoi wanted to sell. In 1652, in order to satisfy this demand and make it safe for European ships at Table Bay, the Dutch East India Company, the trading monopoly established by the Dutch parliament in 1602, founded a permanent outpost there. They hoped it would bring stability to meat prices, as well as give them a monopoly over trade with other European nations' ships. A clay and timber fortress was built that was later replaced by the Castle of Good Hope.

It soon became obvious to Jan van Riebeeck (1619–77), Commander of the Cape, that the amount of fruit and vegetables being produced was inadequate. Therefore he released some of the Company's soldiers from their contracts, allowing them to become independent freeburgher '*boers*' (Dutch for 'farmer'), and providing them with slaves to work land that was purchased from the Khoikhoi whom the settlers named 'Hottentots'. The Khoikhoi, who had initially welcomed the trading opportunities offered by the Europeans, rapidly became disillusioned when they realised they were only permitted to receive luxury items in exchange for their produce. The Europeans feared that, if they gave the local people iron, it would be used to make spears that would be turned against them. Firearms were also withheld. When the Dutch settlers took over some of their traditional grazing lands in 1659, the Khoikhoi rose up in protest. The Boers took refuge in their fortress and, after a stand-off lasting several months during which there was no trade, the Khoikhoi were forced to negotiate. When they pointed out to van Riebeeck that they were the natural owners of the land, he responded that they had lost it in the recent fighting and it was now Dutch. From that point, the Company began to penetrate deeper into the interior.

Following a second Khoi-Dutch war (1673–77), won by the Dutch, the Boer settlement began to expand rapidly. The Company settled the lush pastures of modern-day Paarl and Stellenbosch while encouraging immigration and offering land at a nominal rent. Since the Khoikhoi were unwilling farm labourers and the settlers were unwilling to do the work themselves, slaves were imported. By the end of the eighteenth century, there were 21,000 settlers and 25,000 slaves. Meanwhile, the wealthiest Boers and Company officials were helping themselves to the best farming land, forcing less well-off white settlers to penetrate deeper into the interior. These settlers became known as *trekboers* (from the Dutch word *trek*, meaning 'to pull', as in pulling a wagon), because, being pastoralists, they were always on the move in their ox-drawn wagons. They let their cattle exhaust the grazing of large areas of land before moving on to do the same elsewhere, all the time trading or raiding the sheep and cattle of their Khoikhoi neighbours and rivals. With each *trekboer* son having the right to claim his own land when he came of age, the amount of land claimed by the settlers expanded rapidly.

Some Khoikhoi responded violently – adopting guerrilla tactics – while some simply moved deeper into the interior. Others accepted the status quo and were treated as subservient by the Boers. From 1713, smallpox epidemics, spread from visiting European ships, added to the indigenous people's problems, almost entirely wiping them out. Having lost their way of life, their stock and their livelihood, the Khoikhoi took to stealing the Boers' cattle, to which the Boers responded by forming local militia groups, known as 'commandos'. The Khoikhoi were hunted down, almost to extinction. However, in areas in the north-eastern Cape, where resistance remained strong, they restricted effective Boer settlement throughout the eighteenth century.

The main thrust of Boer settlement was eastwards which allowed some Khoikhoi to move north. Many of these people were, by now, a mixture of Khoikhoi, slave and European genes. Amongst them were fugitives from justice who became leaders of powerful groups of raiders, men such as the German Jan Bloem (1775–1858) and Jager Afrikaner (?-1823). In time, however, the Khoikhoi began to accept their fate, working for the Boers as herdsmen and hunters. Their culture began to disappear as they adopted the language and clothing of the Boers. Many even joined their masters in hunting down their fellow Khoikhoi and later the Xhosa. These Khoikhoi remained a subservient class and, together with freed slaves and people of mixed European, slave and Khoi blood, they began to be known to white settlers in the nineteenth century as 'Cape Coloured'.

By the 1760s, the *trekboers* had arrived at the borders of the fertile, cattle-rich lands occupied by the Xhosa where, in the 1770s, conflict erupted over land. The Khoikhoi had proved a relatively easy opponent, but the Xhosa were a more formidable enemy. War broke out in 1779, ending in stalemate two years later. By the end of the century, feeling that their government had let them down by not supporting their claims, the Boers of the eastern Cape had unsuccessfully rebelled a couple of times, in 1795 and 1799, but by then the British had seized the Cape Colony from the Dutch following Napoleon's occupation of the Seven Provinces of the Netherlands. The Khoikhoi picked this moment to join forces with the Xhosa and rise up against the Boers, raiding their farms. The Third Xhosa War lasted until 1803 by which time the Khoikhoi had lost interest and returned to their masters' farms. However, the Xhosa and

Gqunukhwebe continued to occupy most of the Zuurveld, the land sought by the Boers.

The Southern African Interior

There were numerous states and societies in the interior. By 1500, the pastoral Herero had moved into what is now northern Namibia from modern-day south-eastern Angola and north-western Botswana. The growth in size of their herds forced them to move their small clan-based settlements south into the grassy uplands of central Namibia. Meanwhile, to their east, the Mbanderu expanded towards north-western Botswana and, from southern Namibia, Khoi-speaking Nama clans were moving their sheep northwards to the central highlands. With the Kalahari and Namib deserts providing a barrier to further westward or eastward expansion, therefore, the grazing resources of the Namibian central highlands became highly sought-after and led to the Herero and Nama warring with each other throughout the nineteenth century.

East of the Kalahari, the Sotho-Tswana lived on the Highveld. By the late eighteenth century, in some very large states, the king (*kgosi*) ruled over large capitals inhabited by up to 20,000 people. In agricultural areas near the towns, they cultivated sorghum, millet, pumpkins and beans and beyond those lay grazing lands. They herded sheep and cattle and also hunted. Smaller settlements paid tribute to the *kgosi* who was the spiritual as well as political leader of his people. His performance as ruler was judged on his annual rainmaking efforts between September and November. Failure led to rival claimants emerging. In the early 1600s, the Rolong, Hurutshe, Kwena and Kgatla were the principal Tswana states of the central and western Highveld and they continued to increase their territory until they ruled most of the land between the Vaal River and the Kalahari Desert. The southern Sotho kingdoms were much less organised than those of the northern Sotho – small chiefdoms, mainly, spread across the land that is now Orange Free State and Lesotho. Meanwhile, the Nguni-speaking Zizi had arrived on the southeast Lowveld before the fifteenth century and were organised in small chiefdoms and family-sized settlements that took advantage of the dry, fertile valleys and the variety of arable and grazing opportunities they found.

In the eighteenth century, a number of Nguni chiefdoms, seeking better resources, expanded, absorbing minor chiefdoms in the process. The population was increasing mainly because the unusually heavy rainfall of the second half of the eighteenth century was suitable for the cultivation of maize. Cattle also thrived, more land was brought into cultivation and new grazing lands were created by the cutting down of woodland. Long-distance trade, too – with the Tsonga and the Portuguese – was adding to the growth of the Nguni states. By the late eighteenth century, the Nguni chiefdoms had organised themselves into three centralised kingdoms – the Ngwane of Subhuza (ruled c. 1805–39), the Ndwandwe of Zwide (ruled 1805–20) and the Mthethwa of Dingiswayo (c. 1780–1817). Amongst the chiefdoms that were absorbed by the expanding Mthethwa state was that of the Zulu. Indeed, King Dingiswayo became a mentor to the young Zulu general Shaka who would go on to become Zulu king and one of Africa's greatest warriors. The good years came to an end towards the end of the century when the region was blighted by a prolonged drought.

The Nineteenth Century: Prelude to Conquest

West Africa – Islamic *Jihads*

The Fulbe were a pastoralist people who had spread across West Africa in the seventeenth century. They remained outsiders, however, taking no part in the political life of the area in which they had settled. There was increasing antipathy to them as intruders and they were repressed and subject to crippling taxes and tribute payments. This may be the reason that they turned to Islam, having encountered it through Muslim traders as well as the Tuareg pastoralists who roamed the Sahel. Soon, they were waging *jihad* – holy war – against their repressors.

The first rebellion erupted in the highlands of Futa Jalon, in the area that is now Guinea. In 1725, the Fulbe rose up and, by 1750, they had defeated the farmers who had settled the land. They introduced the *shari'a* – Islamic law. To the south of the Senegal River, in Futa Toro, a new Muslim Fulbe state also emerged following *jihad* in 1769. These successful uprisings encouraged others to follow suit and the early nineteenth century saw a number of *jihads* being fought in the Hausa states in the north of present-day Nigeria where the Fulbe were known as Fulani. As a result of these, the Sokoto caliphate – the largest state in West Africa – was established following a series of *jihads* led by a Muslim scholar Usman dan Fodio (1754–1817). Usman ruled until 1815 before returning to religious life and passing the leadership to his brother, Abdullah (ruled 1815–37), who became Sultan of Gwandu the western part of the state while his son, Muhammad Bello, became Sultan of Sokoto. The empire continued to grow and, by the death of Muhammad Bello, its population numbered ten million people, making it the largest African state until that time.

Meanwhile, in Bornu – formerly known as Kanem-Bornu – situated in the north-east of modern-day Nigeria, a military take-over of this already Islamic state was averted by another remarkable religious leader Muhammad al-Kanemi (1776–1837) who pleaded with the Sultan of Sokoto that, as Bornu had a long and deep Islamic tradition, there was no point in waging *jihad* against it. The leader of Bornu, the *Mai*, was reduced to little more than a ceremonial figurehead while al-Kanemi wielded the real power. On his death, his son Umar ibn Muhammad al-Amin (ruled 1837–81) assumed the leadership. The last in line of the Sayfawa dynasty that had ruled Bornu for seven centuries was defeated in a civil war by Umar and executed in 1846. Umar became outright leader but Bornu's great power and wealth declined. It lost territory in the east to Sokoto and it also lost access to trans-Saharan trade. Towards the end of the nineteenth century, it was seized by Rabih ibn Fadl Allah (1842–1900), a Sudanese military genius who would later lead seven years of fierce resistance to the French.

West of Sokoto there had been other Muslim revolutions. The Fulbe-led Islamic state of Masina had been established in 1818 following a *jihad* in the upper Niger region. Meanwhile, *jihad* in Tukolor, to the west, was led by the Futa Toro Muslim holy man El Hadj Umar Tall (1797–1864) who had been strongly influenced by the *jihad* movements to the east. He succeeded in conquering the Bambara kingdom of Kaarta in what is the western part of modern-day Mali and went on to add the Niger states of Segu and Masina to his Tukolor empire. Conquest and forced conversion led to resistance, especially from the Bambara of the upper Senegal. When Umar died in 1864, the empire was riven with revolt and disagreement amongst his sons, providing the French with the opportunity to take over in the 1880s and 1890s.

The Mandinka Empire

The Mandinka founded an empire that stretched across West Africa. One of its most successful leaders was Samori Touré (c. 1830–1900).

Having undergone military training with the rival Cissé clan and spent two years with the Bérété army – enemies of the Cissé – he returned to his own people the Karama and, in 1861, was appointed *Kélétigui*, or war chief. Samori began creating a professional army of well-trained soldiers, many of them captives, that he employed rather than sold as slaves, thus inculcating loyalty. His army and the friends and relatives he appointed to important positions protected the trade in gold from Bure and cattle from Futa Jalon in which his family was engaged. The wealth from this trade allowed him to import firearms from the coast.

By 1875, he had created a powerful Mandinka kingdom by conquering neighbouring Dyula states. In the meantime, he had become a Muslim while still a young man and he used Islam to unify his kingdom and bring stability to it, making trade easier and creating prosperity for the merchants. In the 1870s, he captured the goldfields in the north and also extended his empire towards Bamako. By the early 1880s, it was the third largest empire in western Africa; only Sokoto and Tukolor were larger. His next enemy would be the French.

Central and East Africa

The slave trade had dominated life in Africa since the late sixteenth century but, although abolition had ended the trade carried out by European countries with America, slaves were still being sent from Angola to Brazil during much of the first half of the nineteenth century. Meanwhile, slavery continued unabated in the interior since labour was needed to produce food for a population that grew as central Africa's fit young men were no longer being sent out of the country in their thousands. Natural resources, already subject to drought and disease, came under pressure, resulting in food shortages. Slaves were viewed as a means of increasing essential food production and were also used to produce the vital exports that allowed Africa to import goods manufactured in Europe's new factories.

The change in the economy also brought political changes as new groups replaced the existing ones. The Chokwe were one such group.

Originating in the remote highland areas of Angola, they were hunters but began to specialise in ivory and the collection of beeswax. They expanded in numbers and territory in the nineteenth century, reaching north and east, towards the outer limits of the forest, and absorbing much of the western part of the declining Lunda Empire. With elephants increasingly difficult to find, due to over-hunting, the Chokwe turned their attention to another much needed commodity – rubber. In Europe, the invention of the pneumatic tyre, firstly for the bicycle and later for the motor car, created a huge demand for rubber which the Chokwe made from latex-producing bushes and creepers. This, however, had devastating results on the forest environment.

Long-distance trading had developed amongst several peoples of the interior as the slave and ivory trades penetrated deeper into their territories. In the nineteenth century, the Ambaquista of Luanda and the Ovimbundu, who inhabited an area deep in Benguela, were the principal exponents of long-distance trade. The Ovimbundu assembled huge caravans that transported goods immense distances, often carried by the slaves that they had once treated as commodities. Amongst those that they supplied were the Chokwe who bought firearms from Ovimbundu traders.

In the 1830s, the Sotho-speaking Kololo, led by Sebetwane (c. 1790–1851) invaded the southern part of the upper Zambesi floodplain, forcing the Lozi royalty who ruled there to flee to the north. Initially, the Kololo did not change much in the way the people were governed. Under Sebetwane's successor Sekeletu (c. 1835–1863), however, the Lozi people became little more than agricultural slaves, burdened by high taxation and the constant threat of being sold to slave-traders in exchange for firearms. In 1864, the Lozi successfully revolted against their usurpers and their aristocracy was re-established. A more militaristic regime ensued, and frequent cattle-raids were carried out against the Ila of the Kafue valley. It has been estimated that, towards the end of the nineteenth century, as many as a third of the Lozi population were servants of the aristocracy or slaves that the *Litunga* (the king) used to dig irrigation canals on the floodplain.

Long-Distance Trade in Eastern Central Africa

By the end of the 1700s, the Lunda kingdom ruled by Kazembe had developed an extensive trading network that reached right across the continent. Kazembe exported ivory, salt, slaves and copper mined in the Copperbelt province of modern Zaire and Zambia. In return, he received firearms, woollen goods from Europe, cloth from India and metal goods manufactured in the factories of Europe. The Bisa in the east, who had provided Kazembe with access to Portuguese traders and settlers in the Zambesi valley, became full-time traders but were victims of frequent raids by the Bemba who came to control much of the northern part of what would become modern Zambia. To the south and east of Lake Malawi the Yao, like the Bemba, became long-distance traders, having formerly been ivory-hunters. They provided the trading link with the Portuguese at the port of Mozambique and they also improved the fortunes of the Swahili port of Kilwa by opening up trading routes to it.

Meanwhile, the *prazeros* – descendants of Portuguese and Afro-Portuguese traders and hunters – used their Chikunda armies, consisting of enslaved captives, to control vast swathes of land, and treated the indigenous peoples as their subjects. They imposed heavy taxation and lived off the food produced by the local people, as did their armies. The *prazeros* took over the ivory trade in the eighteenth century, replacing the declining Maravi empire in that role. They also traded in slaves who were used to transport ivory to the coast as well as serve in their armies. The Chikunda expanded their reach into the middle Zambesi valley, taking what they needed by force.

The Zulu Wars in southern Africa that had driven the Kololo north to invade the upper Zambesi floodplain also drove the Nguni northwards, bringing to the region the entirely new concept, introduced by the Zulus, of centralised military organisation. The Nguni leader, Zwangendaba kaHlatshwayo (ruled c. 1815–48), established a state in the Chipata region of modern-day Zambia, the Mzimba and Karonga districts of modern Malawi and the Matema district of Tanzania, conquering and integrating indigenous people. When Zwangendaba died, his kingdom was engulfed in succession disputes and eventually split into seven separate states, perpetuating the highly-disciplined regimental system of the Zulus in their armies, raiding neighbours and exacting tribute as well as stealing grain and cattle. Their rigid military discipline would later result in the Nguni offering the stoutest resistance to the colonial powers towards the end of the nineteenth century.

The Slave Trade in Central Africa in the Nineteenth Century

The *prazeros* of the lower Zambesi were quick to recognise the lucrative market for slaves and resorted even to selling their own people into slavery as well as their Chikunda armies. This saw the end of smaller *prazos* – or estates – and many disappeared into large *prazos* such as those at Makanga, Massangano and Massingire. These super-*prazos* would present the Portuguese with stiff opposition as they tried to extend their colonial conquests in the 1880s.

It was a dangerous time and raids in formerly prosperous farming areas of modern Malawi and eastern Zambia by the Yao, Nguni and Chikunda led to farming communities across east-central Africa living in stockade villages. Slave trader, plantation owner and governor Hamed bin Muhammed (1837–1905), more commonly known as Tippu Tip, was the most notorious of the Swahili/Arab traders of the central African interior. Employed by a succession of sultans of Zanzibar, he built a trading empire stretching from Luba in the south to the the upper Congo river. By the early 1880s, he commanded an army of several thousand men. Hunting elephants far into the Zaire forest, Tippu Tip and his men displayed scant regard for human life, raiding settlements for food and captives who could be used or sold as slaves. They were put to work in the cultivation of sugar cane, rice and maize that was grown around the towns of Kasongo and Nyangwe.

The Welsh-born American journalist and explorer Henry Morton

Stanley (1841–1904) wrote in his journal about an encounter with one of Tippu Tip's caravans:

> 'Halt at Mpotira, to allow a winding caravan under our escort to come up with hundreds of sheep and goats which they are taking to Tata for trade. A sheep is said to purchase one [tusk of] ivory, 12 slaves purchase an ivory. In Ujiji 6 slaves purchase an ivory.
>
> 'Slaves cost nothing,' said Hamed bin Muhammed [Tippu Tip], 'they only require to be gathered.'
>
> These half-castes of Nyangwe have no cloth or beads or wares of merchandise. They obtain their ivory by robbing…They attack the simple peoples of Nyangwe right and left, 12 or 15 slaves then caught are sold for 35 pounds (16 kilos) of ivory.'

> (H.M. Stanley and A. Neame (ed.), *The Exploration Diaries of H.M. Stanley*, William Kimber, London, 1961; entry for November 7th 1876)

The trade in ivory, firearms and slaves and the violence that came with it dominated the economic life of eastern-central Africa throughout the nineteenth century. A few made great fortunes from it, but the ordinary people enjoyed none of the wealth. Critically, however, the continuation of the slave trade brought persistent turmoil to the region. This gave European nations both the opportunity and the reason to take an even greater interest in Africa. Eventually, they intervened and for the African people this resulted in a different form of slavery; but it was slavery, nonetheless.

Southern Africa

Between about 1815 and 1840, a series of wars raged across the southern African interior, creating turmoil and displacement amongst the indigenous peoples living there. The Nguni of the southeast gave these conflicts the name *Mfecane* (the 'crushing') while the Sotho-Tswana of the Highveld called it *Difaqane* (the 'scattering'). By the late eighteenth century, as we have seen, the Nguni chiefdoms of the north had become three centralised kingdoms – the Ngwane of Sobhuza, the Ndwandwe of Zwide and the Mthethwa of Dingiswayo. The latter federation had absorbed the chiefdom of the Zulu. There was a crisis in the concluding years of the eighteenth century when a generation of stable agricultural production was ended by a major drought. Resources became scarce and survival became precarious. This provided the roots for the terrible conflicts that were to follow, with armies constantly in the field, patrolling their own lands as well as those of weaker chiefdoms who were incorporated into kingdoms in exchange for protection. Three years of intense fighting between 1816 and 1819 resulted in defeat and death for Dingiswayo, great leader of the Mthethwa, but a new leader emerged who would become one of the most influential men in African history.

Shaka kaSenzangakhona (c. 1787–c. 1828), more commonly known as Shaka Zulu, was the son of a chief of the Elangeni tribe, born near modern-day Melmoth in what is now KwaZulu-Natal Province. He served as a warrior under Dingiswayo for around ten years, distinguishing himself in battle. Under his leadership, Shaka's regiments were unbeatable, forcing the Ndwandwe and the northern Nguni north. Shaka expanded his territory over the next decade using innovative military techniques. The army was based on the *ibutho*, an age-based regimental system and was tightly disciplined and closely drilled. His warriors, using a short, stabbing spear, were ruthless and determined. He ruled absolutely, and the leaders of conquered areas were replaced by appointed officials (*indunas*) who answered directly to him. Resistance was ruthlessly suppressed and the populations of entire villages were sometimes massacred. Regimental towns, with a cattle enclosure in the centre, were strategically positioned around Shaka's kingdom and only after serving in the army for a period of time could warriors marry and establish their own homes. They remained liable for call-up, however. Shaka's system dispensed with regional and tribal identities to the extent that during his reign all of his people came to regard themselves as Zulu.

Meanwhile, to the north, the *Mfecane* led to the emergence of new states. The Ngwane of Sbhuza I (ruled c. 1805–c. 1839) founded the future Swazi kingdom north of the Pongola River. In the south of modern-day Mozambique, the Ndwandwe commander, Soshangane (died 1856), formerly one of Shaka's generals, established the state of Gaza. Meanwhile, the Nguni, as has already been mentioned, established themselves on the floodplain of the upper Zambesi.

In 1828, Shaka was assassinated by his half-brother Dingane (ruled 1828–40) and within just ten years the Zulu kingdom was but a shadow of its former self. Dingane was not the military and political genius his brother was, but it is doubtful whether even Shaka could have saved his kingdom from the new developments in southern Africa. In 1837, Boers who had settled in the Cape Colony swarmed onto the Lowveld in search of new land.

Following the warfare and destruction of the *Difiqane,* order began to be restored on the Highveld as strong leaders emerged. Amongst them was Moshoeshoe I (c. 1786–1870), chief of the southern Sotho and founder of the Basuto kingdom. In the early 1820s, Moshoeshoe based himself on the slopes of a mountain east of the upper Caledon river, before moving his growing group of followers to Thaba-Bosiu, a large flat-topped sandstone plateau located in the modern district of Maseru in Lesotho. This afforded him an excellent defensive position. The Sotho state he created there was different to the centralised state established by Shaka, in that it was a confederation of chiefdoms, each of which retained a degree of independence. He offered lesser chiefs protection in return for tribute, the support of their armies and their acknowledgment of his overall authority. His kingdom expanded rapidly as a result. Moshoeshoe adroitly recognised the power of several other states, paying tribute, for instance, to both Shaka and Matiwane's Ngwane. He also recognised the wisdom of maintaining good relations with the whites of the Cape Colony, inviting missionaries to work in his kingdom. It was a relationship he hoped might deter damaging raids by the Griqua and Kora who lived in the north of the Colony, by providing him with access to firearms and horses. It paid off and his kingdom developed into a formidable power in the region.

On the Highveld the Ndebele kingdom was established by Mzilikazi (ruled c. 1823–68). He organised it in the Zulu manner with age regiments and regimental villages. Like Shaka's warriors, the Ndebele were ruthless in the collection of tribute. Eventually, however, a number of attacks from the south, the most serious by a combination of Boers, Griqua and Rolong, drove the Ndebele from the Highveld. By 1840, they had retreated north of the Limpopo where they conquered the Shona Rozwi state and re-established a power base.

The Arrival of the British in Southern Africa

The Dutch East India Company had established the Cape Colony in 1652. Occupied by the British in 1795, in order to prevent its seizure by revolutionary France which had occupied the Netherlands, it was returned to Dutch control in 1803. In 1806, with the French resurgent in the Netherlands, it was once again occupied by the British. In 1814, the Dutch government formally handed the colony over to the British under the terms of the Convention of London.

Initially, British occupation appeared to be beneficial to the Dutch, as new markets were opened up for Dutch wine-makers of the Western Cape and a greater number of British ships anchored at the Colony. The real divisions were over labour. With slavery abolished, the British tightened the regulations concerning free labour. The so-called 'Hottentot Code' of 1809 stipulated that all Khoikhoi and 'free-black' men had to carry 'passes' that bore their address and the name of their employer. Any found not to be in possession of a pass were contracted to the nearest colonist who required labour. On the other hand, employers were obliged to provide contracts of employment and employees had redress to the courts if their contract was breached or they were physically abused. Missionaries at the Cape opposed Boer oppression of employees and succeeded in getting the British to dispense with the 'Hottentot Code'. Workers were thereby free to go wherever they liked and to work for whomever they wanted.

The Boers resented these moves, leading a large number to

undertake a trek northwards in the 1830s and 1840s, in the large-scale migration known as the 'Great Trek', often seen as the definitive moment in the development of Afrikaner nationalism. The British brought a standing army to Cape Town which served to keep the *trekboers* in line but was also of use to the settlers engaged in the struggle with the Xhosa for the lands of the Zuurveld, in the Eastern Cape. The Dutch had already fought three wars with the Xhosa and now it was the turn of the British. The Xhosa were heavily defeated by a brutal British effort during which they pushed their enemy out of the Zuurveld altogether and beyond the Fish River to the east. This put pressure on the Xhosa already occupying this area and before long the two groups were at war. When the British intervened in this civil war in 1818, the Fifth Xhosa War followed. The result was that the indigenous people were pushed even further east.

The British attempted to create a barrier between the Xhosa and the Zuurveld by giving permission to a group of Khoikhoi and 'coloured' or mixed race farmers to settle there but soon the Xhosa were back in the area, fighting with *trekboer* settlers who had also arrived in the region in defiance of British orders. The subsequent Sixth Xhosa War resulted in the Xhosa being pushed further east and the British annexing more of their territory to the west of the river Kei. The Boers and British land speculators, expecting this new land to be opened up for settlement, were disappointed when the British handed it back to the Xhosa. Still more Boers joined the Great Trek north.

The Great Trek was, in fact, a series of small, individual treks that resulted in a number of trekker republics on the Highveld that were all suspicious of each other. They were free, however, of British control and had immense swathes of land to claim as their own. Initially, in the treks of the 1830s and 1840s, what land they occupied depended largely on the absence of indigenous peoples or, at least, the absence of any resistance from those that were there. The areas that had been depopulated by the *Mfecane/Difaqane* were ideal. Some peoples, such as the Rolong, saw benefits in having the Boers around, believing their firepower and horses would help them against their old enemies the Ndebele who had recently driven them from their homeland. Their faith in Boer strength was rewarded when the Ndebele were driven out. But the Boers took over the former Ndebele lands, founding their principal settlements to the north and south of the middle Vaal, and the Rolong in the area found themselves subject to taxation and demands for free labour.

In the Lowveld, after conflict with the Zulus, the Boers decided to found their 'republic' of Natalia away from the densely populated Zulu homelands. In 1843, however, Natal, as Natalia had become known, was annexed by the British, forcing most of its Boer inhabitants northwards into Transorangia – later known as Orange Free State – and the Transvaal. These republics were recognised by the British at the 1852 Sand River and 1854 Bloemfontein conferences. Elsewhere on the Highveld, Moshoeshoe's Sotho kingdom mounted fierce resistance to Boer occupation. In a series of conflicts in the 1850s and 1860s, however, the Orange Free State Boers slowly began to gain territory at his expense. To save his kingdom from extinction, Moshoeshoe asked the British to annex it.

The best land of the eastern Cape was sold to white settlers who used it to graze Merino sheep. Xhosa found it impossible to eke out an existence and began to depend, largely, on the poor wages paid for working on the settlers' farms. In Natal, where most of the settler-owners were absentee farmers, the Africans worked as peasant farmers, renting their land from the whites. In most places, however, they were expected to provide free labour to the Boers when it was required. British merchants at the coastal ports became wealthy due to the demand from the people of the southern African interior, both black and white, for firearms and luxuries manufactured in European factories. In return, skins, ivory and ostrich feathers were exported.

By 1870, the white man was firmly ensconced in the areas that had experienced the turmoil of the *Mfecane/Difaqane*. In other parts of the interior, however, Africans had strengthened themselves with the acquisition of firepower and major and costly military effort would be required to extend settlement further into the interior. It would take the discovery of valuable minerals such as diamonds and gold in the 1870s and 1880s to suddenly make that effort worthwhile.

North and North-East Africa

Although part of the Ottoman Empire in the early part of the nineteenth century, the Turkish rulers of North Africa operated fairly independently. Even so, their authority did not extend far beyond the coastal strip.

Algeria

The French had been engaged in disputes with the ruler of Algeria, the *dey*, for decades and, in 1827, diplomatic relations were finally broken. In 1830, France invaded, ostensibly to stop piracy, but in reality in an effort to boost the image of the French monarchy at home. The nomadic and semi-nomadic clans and Muslim brotherhoods of Algeria had been rivals for centuries, but the French threat and the possibility of the imposition of an alien religion, culture and legal system united them. At least the Turks had been Muslim, after all. They launched a *jihad* – a holy war that would last for fifty years, one of the fiercest wars of resistance against colonial rule on the continent.

The early leader of the Algerian resistance was the Islamic scholar, Sufi and political and military leader Abd al-Qadir (1808–1883) who united all the disparate elements of the Algerian resistance into a single entity. Ultimately, however, the French won with an army that, by 1850, numbered 100,000 men. In the process it lost many thousands of troops. Algerian losses were even greater, in the hundreds of thousands. Abd al-Qadir was himself captured and exiled in 1847, but Algerian resistance continued until 1879 when the French could at last consider themselves to be victorious.

Arab-Berber farmers and pastoralists were driven from their land as white settlers from both France and Spain began to arrive. By 1871, the *colons*, as the settlers were called, numbered 130,000 and by 1900 there were a million. They owned most of the arable land but were mainly absentee farmers, living in the cities and leaving poorly-paid and unfairly taxed indigenous farmers to work the land. French law replaced Islamic law and restrictions, reminiscent of those imposed on the indigenous peoples of southern Africa, were imposed on Algerians who continued to seethe with resentment.

Egypt

Muhammed Ali, often regarded as the founder of modern Egypt, was actually born in the Ottoman province of Albania, arriving in Egypt as a soldier in the Ottoman army that drove the French from the country in 1801. He soon became *pasha* (viceroy) of Egypt, a position that he rapidly consolidated. He gained the support of the population by styling himself the champion of the people and by dispensing with the corrupt practices prevalent under the old Mamluk rule. Using European models as his template, rather than African or Asian ones, he streamlined the economy, creating a trained, salaried civil service and a modern professional army. His regime, however, was just as unforgiving to the Egyptian *fellahin* as all the others that had preceded it. Taxation was punitive and, if they were unable to pay, their land was confiscated. As ever, they were forced to work for nothing and were conscripted into the army. Resistance was ruthlessly suppressed. Muhammed Ali created what was, in effect, a state monopoly. All producers had to sell their goods to the state which then re-sold them, retaining any profit. He also developed a weapons industry with Cairo factories producing cannons and muskets and built a shipyard in Alexandria to create an Egyptian navy. Schools and hospitals were constructed and students were sent abroad to study.

The Mamluks were disposed of in 1811 when Muhammed Ali ordered the massacre of several hundred Mamluk *beys*. The remainder fled the country and the state seized their estates. In 1821, the Egyptian army invaded the Sudan, to crush the Mamluks who had fled there and to find slaves. During the 1820s, they extended control southwest of Khartoum and conquered the region of southern Sudan where elephants, and therefore ivory, were plentiful. The new Egyptian navy reasserted Ottoman power in the Red Sea, leading to a revival of trade by that route to the Indian Ocean. He also defeated the Wahida clans of central Arabia who had long occupied the holy cities of Mecca and Medina, opening the way for pilgrims once again to visit them. Eventually, Muhammed Ali achieved his objective of having the Ottoman sultan recognise his family as hereditary rulers of Egypt. He had created a dynasty.

After his death in 1849, French and British influence in Egypt increased. The British had begun to use the Red Sea as a shorter route to India, investing heavily in the construction of a railway from Alexandria to Cairo and Suez. The French, meanwhile, began the construction of the Suez Canal, linking the Mediterranean to the Red Sea. It opened in 1869, by which time an increasing amount of Egypt's trade was being carried by European ships and Egypt's indebtedness to the European powers had begun to create difficulties. In 1876, Muhammed Ali's grandson Isma'il Pasha (ruled 1863–79) had the unenviable task of facing up to the fact that Egypt was bankrupt. The British and the French, worried about the threat this might pose to their huge investments in the country, deposed Isma'il, and took over the country's finances. Faced with an army coup in 1881, the British, with the full support of the French, occupied Egypt.

The Sudan and the Mahdist State
Egyptian rule over the Sudan created huge resentment amongst the Sudanese. In 1881, a holy man from Dongola, Muhammad Ahmad (1844–85), claimed to be the redeemer of the Islamic faith – the *Mahdi* – and declared a *jihad* against the invaders. His call for holy war received an enthusiastic response from a Sudanese people burdened by heavy taxation that added to their frustration at the attempts by the British General Charles George Gordon (1833–85) to suppress the slave trade, from which Sudanese traders had made fortunes for centuries. There was outrage too at the blatant corruption of their new overlords, their lack of Islamic observance and an administration in which Christian Europeans held important positions. The Mahdist forces won impressive early victories against the powerful modern

armies that faced them and, in 1885, they took Khartoum, killing General Gordon and massacring Egyptian soldiers and officials who had remained in the city.

The Sudanese were stunned five months later, however, when Muhammad Ahmad died – the Mahdi was supposed to be immortal. He was replaced in 1885 by Abdullah Ibn-Mohammed (c. 1846–99). 'The Khalifa' ('successor'), as he was known, governed well but a great deal of effort went into fighting the Sudan's neighbours – Egypt and Ethiopia. Eventually, in 1898, the Egyptians and British routed the Sudanese army at the Battle of Omdurman in which twenty thousand Sudanese troops died. The Mahdist state was finished and the Sudan, like Egypt, became virtually a British colony.

Ethiopia

By the nineteenth century, the Ethiopian emperor was little more than the nominal head of a federation in which individual rulers asserted their independence. In 1855, however, the governor of the western province of Qwara Lij Kassa Haylu (ruled 1855–68) seized the throne. Taking the name Tewodros II, he re-imposed central authority on Ethiopia. Tewodros appointed district governors and judges, reducing the power of local nobles as well as his reliance on tribute paid to him by those nobles. He created a well-drilled, modern, professional, national army that he used ruthlessly to suppress rebellions between 1855 and 1861. However, he made the fatal error of abolishing many of the privileges of the Ethiopian Church and appropriated many Church estates.

In 1868, after he had arrested the local British consul following a minor dispute, a British army of 30,000 men was sent into Ethiopia in a disproportionate show of force. Without the support of the Church and facing the antipathy of his people, Tewodros's army deserted, leaving him with a mere 4,000 men to defend his position. He committed suicide rather than be taken prisoner and the British withdrew from Ethiopia.

Under Tewodros' successors, the regional aristocracy regained its former power and Ethiopia once again reverted to feudalism. One of these, Menelik II (ruled 1889–1913), was a moderniser who, amongst other things, built Ethiopia's first hospital, founded its first bank and introduced a postal system. He expanded his empire in the south but, in the north, he faced the imperial aspirations of the Italians who had colonised the coastal state of Eritrea and were now eyeing Ethiopia. He won a resounding victory over them at the Battle of Adowa in 1896, leaving Ethiopia to retain its independence as the European superpowers carved up the rest of the African continent.

The Nineteenth Century: Conquest and Colonisation

Explorers and Missionaries

In the middle of the nineteenth century, European explorers began to penetrate the West African interior. It had been ignored for centuries, partly because of the risk of disease and death but also because there was little reason to venture beyond the safety of the coastal strip. The trade in slaves worked well and there was no need to change it.

Christian missionaries followed, seeking to spread the word of God and realising that the interior held a huge number of potential converts. For the first seventy-five years or so of the nineteenth century, however, governments were reluctant to become involved in anything away from their coastal enclaves and imperial aspirations were far from their thoughts. There was little to be gained, they believed, and quite a lot to lose.

The movement for the abolition of the slave trade had revived interest in Africa, however. Replacing that shameful trade with legitimate commerce became an aspiration for abolitionists and, for that to happen, a greater knowledge of the African continent was required. Religion was also believed to be a way to supplant the slave trade. The evangelical churches that had arisen in Europe in the previous century, to assuage the grinding poverty of the Industrial Revolution, created their own missionary societies. But little was known of the traditional religions that Christianity would come up against in the interior – Europeans on the coasts knew nothing of life inland. In the first half of the nineteenth century, missionaries deduced, therefore, that the most effective way to get their message heard would be to convert and train Africans to be clergymen.

Meanwhile, African rulers were anxious to benefit from the skills of the European missionaries and their African acolytes, and to obtain the luxury goods to which they had access. More often than not, therefore, they converted to Christianity for practical, rather than spiritual, reasons.

An enormous number of explorers travelled to Africa. Their reasons were various – some were engaged in scientific enquiry; some were adventurers or seekers of fame or fortune. All were certain, however, that their explorations would help to drive trade in the future that would ultimately benefit Europe. In 1788, the African Association had been formed by a group of wealthy Englishmen who wanted to dispatch an expedition to Timbuktu to investigate the course of the Niger river in the hope that there might be gold reserves in the area. Mungo Park (1771–1806) was the association's first explorer. He visited the Niger twice, but died during his second attempt to follow the course of the river to the sea. In 1827, the Frenchman René Caillié (1799–1838) became the first European to reach Timbuktu and return safely. In 1830 two Cornish brothers John (1807–1839) and Richard Lander (1804–1834) followed the Niger from the town of Bussa to the sea, proving that there was a navigable river that flowed deep into the heart of Africa.

Malaria, however, would maintain Africa's reputation as the 'White Man's Grave' for another two decades until the discovery of quinine's efficacy against the disease quickened the pace of European exploration. Other potential trading arteries – the upper Nile, the Zambesi and the Congo rivers – were also explored during the 1850s, 1860s and 1870s. British explorers Sir Richard Burton (1821–90), John Hanning Speke (1827–64) and James Augustus Grant (1827–92) located the source of the White Nile at Lake Victoria Nyanza, while, further south, Scottish explorer, missionary and fervent advocate of the abolition of slavery David Livingstone (1813–73) crossed the continent from east to west and back again. He spent his last years exploring Lake Malawi and the waterways of southern-central Africa. Henry Morton Stanley carried on Livingstone's work by following the Congo River from its upper tributary, the Lualaba, to its entry into the

Atlantic Ocean at Boma in the modern-day Democratic Republic of the Congo. To the north, the German explorers Heinrich Barth (1821–65) and Gustav Nachtigal (1834–85) were following the trade routes of the Sahara and the Sahel.

As explorers opened up potential trade routes and European merchants pushed their contacts deeper into the interior, European governments slowly began to take interest. The French had established a colony along the banks of the Senegal river as far as Medina while the British declared the Fante states – located in modern-day Ghana – a Crown Colony following a challenge by the Ashanti Confederacy to the British trading monopoly on West Africa's Gold Coast. The British consolidated their position with a victory over the Ashanti in 1874. Around this time, British merchants were also taking control of the trade on the lower Niger.

When Stanley announced his 'discovery' of the Congo River, the Belgian King Leopold II (ruled 1865–1909) commissioned him to return to the mouth of the river to build a road linking Boma with Malebo Pool. It was the start of the king's colonisation plans. It was also the start of the so-called 'scramble for Africa'.

The 'Scramble for Africa'

Although they had shown little or no interest in Africa beyond their enclaves on the coast for the past 400 years, by 1898 the European states had swallowed up almost the entire continent. The speed at which this occurred was certainly puzzling, leading one eminent British historian of the time, Sir John Seeley, to say that the empire had been acquired 'in a fit of absence of mind' (*The Expansion of England: Two Courses of Lectures* London, Macmillan, 1883).

It had been made possible to a large extent by European technological developments such as steamboats, railways and the telegraph, plus the decisive factor – modern firearms. Africans had no answer to weapons such as the magazine repeating rifle or Hiram S. Maxim's (1840–1916) Maxim gun, the first machine gun and 'the weapon most associated with [British] imperial conquest' (*A History* of the Twentieth Century: Volume One; 1900–1933, Martin Gilbert, William Morrow and Company, New York). Although Africans had long been able to acquire firearms, none ever managed to get their hands on a Maxim gun. British anti-imperialist poet Hilaire Belloc summed it up in a famous couplet:

'Whatever happens we have got
The Maxim-gun; and they have not.'

Europeans justified their African land-grabbing by claiming that it was their duty to bring civilisation – or, at least, the European version of it – to Africa. The European had a moral duty to 'improve' the life of the African, a sentiment characterised as the 'white man's burden' in Rudyard Kipling's 1899 poem of the same name written to celebrate Queen Victoria's Diamond Jubilee. Of course, those who refused to accept the new culture were ruthlessly dealt with.

France, Spain, Great Britain, Portugal and the Netherlands had long had empires, but there were newly unified nations who wanted their share of the spoils. In January 1871, the numerous states of Germany had unified under the political leadership of Chancellor Otto von Bismarck (1815–98). Germany immediately assumed imperialistic ambitions under Bismarck's policy of *Weltpolitik* (World Politics) in order to prove its military superiority to the rest of Europe. It looked to Africa to fulfil those ambitions. Five years earlier, Italy had also unified and developed a belief that she deserved her own overseas empire, just like the older nations. The Italians first considered Tunisia, but that was already the object of French imperial ambition. Its attention shifted, therefore, to Ethiopia and the Horn of Africa.

Of course, trade was one of the principal reasons for the 'Scramble for Africa'. Britain, the 'workshop of the world', had pioneered the industrial revolution and was Europe's leading industrial nation until the second half of the nineteenth century. British goods, shipped to customers by the world's biggest merchant navy, dominated Africa's imports. By 1870, however, Britain's advantage was being eroded as industry in France, Germany and the United States began to catch up, bringing the problem of over-production. With European markets unable to consume this over-production, manufacturers began to look around for new markets. Africa provided the solution and European cloth, clothes, alcohol, weapons and metal manufactured goods started to flood into the continent. This, in turn, led to protectionism. France and Germany realised that the way to beat the British was to create colonies or enclaves from which British and other goods could be banned or, at least, have heavy import duties imposed on them.

Another factor which contributed to the 'scramble' was the belief that there must be a wealth of raw materials and precious minerals in this vast continent. This was confirmed when, in 1867, a small girl picked up a glittering stone from the dry bed of the Orange River in southern Africa. It turned out to be a 21-carat diamond. Four years later, 5,000 miners from all over the world were working claims at Kimberley, many successfully. The race was on and the British government realised that the only way it could profit from it was by taxation and duty which meant incorporating the area into its empire.

Of course, Africans themselves played a part in the 'scramble'. Firstly, there were often long-standing local rivalries between African states that could be played off against each other by the Europeans. Many rulers signed treaties with the Europeans in order to gain protection against their enemies. It did not take long, however, to realise that this 'protection' involved their complete submission to their so-called ally.

Britain and the Suez Canal

In 1882, there was a danger that Egyptian nationalists, led by Colonel Ahmed Orabi (1841–1911), would seize control of the Suez Canal. Britain could ill afford to lose this strategically vital waterway that was so important to its expansionist aims and immediately dispatched a force that routed the Egyptian army at a battle fought near Tel el-Kebir. Britain occupied Egypt, taking control of the Suez Canal. To protect the canal, the waters of the Nile had to be secure and the British were naturally concerned that the source of the river was 4,000 miles away in the heart of Africa. Somewhat reluctantly, they secured control of more than a million square miles of East Africa and the Sudan.

The Berlin Conference (1884–85)

The 'scramble for Africa' was, effectively, formalised by the Berlin Conference, called for by Portugal and organised by Bismarck. He invited representatives of Austria–Hungary, Belgium, Denmark, France, the United Kingdom, Italy, the Netherlands, Portugal, Russia, Spain, Sweden – Norway – who were in a union until 1905 – the Ottoman Empire, and the United States which declined the invitation.

The objective of the conference was to reach agreement about the sharing out of the African continent. It did not actually establish colonial boundaries but it did away with 'spheres of influence', something that the British had been claiming in various areas, much to the annoyance of Bismarck. A colonial claim would only be recognised if the country involved was 'effectively occupied' by the country making the claim. Just to make sure the British understood this principle, only days after the conference had ended Bismarck proclaimed a German protectorate in the middle of Britain's East African 'sphere of influence'. It became known as German East Africa (later Tanganyika and now Tanzania) and could be claimed as being 'effectively occupied' because a German agent had travelled there and concluded treaties with a number of local leaders.

There was still a long way to go, however. Although a number of European treaties of 1890–91 confirmed many of the African colonial boundaries, the European powers were patently failing to abide by the principle of 'effective occupation'. And of course, during the coming decade, Africans were unwilling to give up their independence without a struggle.

The French in West and North-Central Africa

In the 1850s and 1860s, the French, using a well-drilled, well-equipped and locally-recruited Senagalese army, extended their territory up the Senegal valley in order to secure French trade. This was followed by an aggressive campaign of colonisation across West Africa. Opposed to their endeavours in the western Sudan were the Tukolor Empire, ruled by Ahmadu Seku (ruled 1864–92), and the Mandinka Empire ruled by Samori Ture. Ahmadu initially tried diplomacy, signing a treaty with the French that ostensibly recognised his empire. The French, however, had little interest in honouring it. In 1889, when they attacked Tukolor fortresses on the border, Ahmadu's forces put up stiff resistance but were finally defeated in 1893. Ahmadu was deposed and replaced by his brother.

Many of Ahmadu's forces moved south into Mandinka territory to join Samori in his independence struggle. His army, of 33,000 men and elite cavalry, possessed an enduring national pride which dated back to the Malian empire and was an altogether different proposition to the Tukolor soldiers. Again, French treaties were little more than delaying tactics, and the French invaded in 1891. Samori adopted a 'scorched earth' policy that devastated his empire but forced the French, short of supplies, to withdraw in 1892. After he had moved his entire empire eastwards to the northern borders of present-day Ghana and Côte d'Ivoire, and had had a request for protectorate status denied by the British, Samori at last had no option but to face the French. He won several battles but eventually his army was defeated, the victim not of French firepower but of famine. Samori surrendered and was sent into exile in Gabon.

In central Sudan, resistance was led by the warlord and slave trader Rabin ibn Fadl Allah (c 1842–1900), a disciple of the Mahdi, who had conquered Bornu. In 1900, two French armies attacked Bornu, killing Rabih but leaving his son to continue the resistance. He, too, was killed by the French in 1901, after he had been denied, like Samori, protectorate status by the British. Dahomey fell to the French Senagalese army in 1894 and Côte d'Ivoire became a French colony in 1893.

The British in West Africa

Britain declared a colony in the coastal Fante states, having established a trading monopoly along the Gold Coast in the early 1870s. In 1874, in order to assert their coastal authority, they invaded the lands of the Ashanti in the interior, defeating them and destroying their capital, Kumasi. To avoid the costs of colonial administration, however, they quickly withdrew. But, in order to prevent the French making inroads in the region, they again invaded in 1895, proclaiming a British Protectorate over much of the area that is now Ghana. In 1900, the Ashanti rose again, almost defeating the British, but reinforcements secured a British victory and the colony of the Gold Coast was proclaimed.

Following the Berlin Conference, Britain declared a Protectorate over the Niger Delta. A British company, the National African Company, led by Sir George Goldie (1846–1925), had developed a highly lucrative monopoly over palm-oil exports from the region and the British government issued it with a royal charter, giving it permission to govern the lower Niger on behalf of Great Britain. Now named the Royal Niger Company, it kept African traders out of the palm-oil trade by force and merchant princes, reluctant to trade on the terms the British offered, were quickly deposed. By 1902, the immense swathe of land that is modern Nigeria had been brought under British control, much of it by force.

The Congo Basin

In 1880, the French explorer Pierre de Brazza (1852–1905) concluded a treaty with the Tio chief that de Brazza claimed gave the sovereign rights of the chiefdom to France. It is likely that the chief was merely seeking protection from the advances being made at that time by Stanley on behalf of King Leopold of Belgium, using slave labour to build his road from Boma to the Malebo Pool. This treaty and others were used by the French at the Berlin Conference to claim the lands that lay to the north of the lower Congo. In the early 1890s, de Brazza was sent back to Africa where he signed more treaties, creating the French colonies of Gabon, Moyen ('Middle') Congo and Ubangui-Chari which lay in the area of the modern Central African Republic.

In 1865, Leopold II became king of the Belgians. Leopold was fascinated by Africa and determined to create a Belgian empire there. 'I do not want to miss a good chance of getting us a slice of this magnificent African cake,' he is reported to have said (*The Scramble for Africa: White Man's Conquest of the Dark Continent From 1876 to 1912*, Thomas Pakenham, Avon Books, New York, 1992). He hired Henry Morton Stanley to make treaties with African chiefs in the area now known as the Democratic Republic of the Congo which granted full sovereignty over their lands to the International African Society. This masqueraded as a scientific and philanthropic organisation, but was, in fact, a private holding company for the king. Leopold lobbied the kings, queens, statesmen and humanitarians of Europe in pursuit of his goal and, at the Berlin Conference, he was eventually granted sovereignty over his 'Congo Free State' which encompassed an area roughly seventy-six times the size of Belgium. It was his personal fiefdom, his authority imposed with merciless efficiency by his private army, the *Force Publique*.

Portugal and Angola

In the midst of all this manoeuvring, Portugal, a poor country in European terms, was relatively insignificant but this made her all the more reluctant to lose what foothold she did have in Africa, and more eager to exploit the new markets there. Portuguese manufacturers and industrialists encouraged their government to pursue colonial ambitions in the Angolan interior and, lacking the wealth to send in large bodies of troops, the only option was to follow the example of others and exploit age-old rivalries between Africans. It worked, although there were enclaves that remained outside the Portuguese tax-collecting capability until well into the twentieth century, mainly because the huge demand for rubber had provided some of those who lived there with the means to acquire firearms. Only when the rubber trade declined, around 1910, and the ban on sales of guns to Africans was introduced in 1912 did they finally prevail.

The British and the Germans in East Africa

Germany faced stiff opposition from the people of the Tanganyikan interior, and their caravans had to be heavily guarded. Meanwhile, the Hehe in southern-central Tanganyika fought a guerrilla campaign until 1898 when their leader committed suicide rather than face likely capture. Other areas, too, put up stout resistance and the Yao in the southeast fought until 1899. The problems had not gone away, however, and the unrest known as the 'Maji Maji' rising would trouble the Germans again in the early years of the new century. The Heligoland-Zanzibar treaty of 1890 between Britain and Germany had given Germany the North Sea island of Heligoland – a British possession since 1814 – in return for territory in modern Namibia and control over the coast of Dar es Salaam. Furthermore, the area covered by modern Uganda became part of the British Empire, the British handing it to a private company, the Imperial British East Africa Company (IBEAC). A force under Captain Frederick Lugard (1858–1945) persuaded Kabaka Mwanga of Buganda, the region's most powerful kingdom, to acknowledge British authority and the British government took over from the IBEAC in 1894. The Baganda had proved extremely helpful to the British in their conquest of the region and, for that reason, the entire territory was named 'Uganda'. In Kenya, which the British government took over from the IBEAC in 1895, it took nine months to quell resistance.

Britain's Central African Protectorate

In 1889, in an attempt to frustrate Portuguese efforts to prevent British traders gaining access to the region around Lake Nyasa and the Shire Valley, Britain declared the Central African Protectorate, re-naming it Nyasaland (Malawi after independence) in 1897. British explorer Sir Harry Johnston (1858–1927) was appointed administrator and, for most of the 1890s, he was at war ostensibly to suppress the slave trade, but in reality to conquer the area – fighting against the Yao from 1891–95, the Swahili and the Chewa in 1895, and the Nguni from 1895–99. One British official compared Johnston's tactics of presenting each ruler with the choice of signing a treaty and agreeing to pay taxation or face attack and probable death as: 'Treaty or compulsion; your money or your life'. Soon, these tactics assured British authority over the territory as well as the pacification of the Bemba and Nguni of north-east Rhodesia.

The Portuguese in Mozambique

The name 'Mozambique' was first applied to a small coral island at the mouth of Mossuril Bay but was gradually extended to cover all the Portuguese colonies on the African east coast. In the last two decades of the nineteenth century, the Portuguese faced stiff and prolonged resistance to their rule and especially their taxation from a variety of well-armed peoples of the region – the Gaza Empire, the Barwe kingdom, and the large *prazos* of the Zambezi valley amongst them. In 1894, after the British and the Portuguese drew up a treaty that located most of the Gaza Empire within Portuguese control, Gaza warriors attacked the Portuguese coastal town of Lourenço Marques. They were defeated and the Gaza ruler Ngungunyane (ruled c. 1884–95) was taken prisoner. The Portuguese relied heavily on local troops to enforce their authority in much of Mozambique. This often resulted in situations that were more like civil wars than a war of conquest by an external power as longstanding local rivalries rose to the surface.

The Germans and Namibia

In Namibia the Germans were also able to exploit local rivalries as they sought, under the pretext of protecting their missionaries and traders, to establish a colonial empire in Africa. In 1884, they proclaimed a protectorate over an area stretching from the Orange

River in the south to the Kunene River in the north. Six years later, they moved inland onto the dry grassland of the central plateau where the Nama and Herero peoples had been at war with each other for a century. The Germans adroitly exploited this bitter rivalry, offering a treaty of protection to the Herero against the Nama.

However, the Nama chief Hendrik Witbooi (ruled 1888–1905) was wise to the tricks of colonising nations, writing a remarkable letter to his rival the Herero chief Maherero (ruled c. 1860s-90):

'You think you will retain your independent Chieftainship after I have been destroyed... but my dear Kaptein you will eternally regret your action in having handed over to the White man the right to govern your country. After all our war is not as serious as you think... but this thing you have done, to surrender yourself to the Government of the White man, will be a burden that you will carry on your shoulders. You call yourself Supreme Chief, but when you are under another's control you are merely a subordinate chief.'

(*The Diary of Hendrik Witbooi*, Van Riebeeck Society)

Maherero was not to be swayed, however, and the Germans launched an attack on Witbooi at Gibeon. Witbooi and his men broke out and proceeded to wage guerrilla warfare but the Germans eventually overcame them in 1894.

Meanwhile, during a succession dispute following Maherero's death, the Germans established a garrison in the Herero capital, declaring that they recognised Samuel Maherero (ruled 1890–1917) as chief. They then proceeded to allocate land for white settlement without consulting with the new chief or his people. By 1900, the entire area of south-west Africa had been conquered, although a great deal of conflict would follow in the first decade of the new century.

South-Central and Southern Africa

The southern African 'mineral revolution' that was launched with the discovery of diamonds in 1870 transformed the region, taking it on a vastly different trajectory to the rest of the continent. The diamond fields were located to the north of the Cape Colony but the land on which they were found was the subject of dispute, claimed not only by Orange Free State and the Transvaal but also by the local Griqua, Tswana and Kora people. A British court of enquiry found in favour of the Griqua whose chief had, coincidentally, requested British Protectorate status in the face of Boer threats and so the British handily annexed the world's richest diamond fields, designating the colony Griqualand West.

In the 1880s, one company came to dominate the diamond fields. Financed by the private investment banking company N.M. Rothschild & Sons English businessman Cecil Rhodes (1853–92), who had already made a fortune from diamonds during the previous decade, founded De Beers. By the last year of the decade, the company had bought out all the other mining companies and created a monopoly, allowing it to pay African workers low wages and force them to live in fenced-in compounds, away from their families. Naturally, the region was rapidly transformed. Tens of thousands of people arrived who needed to be housed and fed, providing a financial boost for local farmers, black and white. This created greater competition for agricultural land, however, and the working conditions of farm workers and labourers deteriorated. With 55,000 miners needed, the new phenomenon of migrant labour emerged, although many of the workers made the long journey simply in order to earn the cost of a gun to use against white settlement.

The mineral revolution brought an increase in European colonial ambition and a more aggressive approach to white settlement. The British led the way with their intention to amalgamate southern Africa's white-controlled states into a federation. To do this, however, and to provide security for white settlement, they had to dispose of the remaining African kingdoms in the region. In 1877–78, in pursuit of this objective, the British fought the ninth war with the Xhosa, facing resolute resistance that was sufficient to make them decide against seizing any more land from them.

In 1879, the British took on Cetshwayo's (ruled 1872–79) Zulu kingdom but were heavily defeated by 20,000 Zulu warriors at the Battle of Isandlwana, despite a huge discrepancy in weaponry. This ended the idea of a federation, although the British finally defeated and captured Cetshwayo eight months later, after importing thousands of reinforcements. The Zulu kingdom would dissolve into internecine rivalry in the 1880s and, ravaged by famine, Zululand finally became a British colony in 1887. Meanwhile, with the Transvaal facing economic ruin, Britain annexed it in 1877. The Boers, however, resenting the British presence and especially British taxation, rebelled in 1880, initiating the First Boer War which ended with a truce in March 1881. The British withdrew, giving the Transvaal back its independence, but with Britain still retaining elements of its governance.

The mineral revolution entered its second phase in 1886 when gold was discovered at the Witwatersrand range of hills in central Transvaal. It was a massive find with the area becoming the source of forty per cent of all the gold ever mined. Some of that gold was ploughed into the transformation of Johannesburg from a few scruffy tents into the largest city south of the Sahara. The discovery also signalled a change in the balance of power as southern Africa's economic powerhouse moved from Britain's Transvaal to the Boer republic. To mine the deposits, however, required significant investment and, by the 1890s, the goldfields were dominated by a handful of big companies which had bought all other claims. Amongst them was Cecil Rhodes' Consolidated Goldfields. As with the diamond fields, there was competition for land in the region as Johannesburg provided a huge new market for agricultural produce. White settlement increased at the expense of black farmers who were forced into tenancy agreements and the provision of free labour to work on land that had belonged to them just a short time ago. The Transvaal government benefited greatly from the gold mines, imposing heavy taxes and using the revenue to create a large, standing army with which they made further gains in the northern Highveld. By 1898, the Boers controlled territory stretching north to the Limpopo.

Zimbabwe

Cecil Rhodes next turned his attention to the Zimbabwe plateau where he and his investors were convinced they would find gold. Making it even more attractive was the fact that it lay beyond the reach of Boer tax-collectors. The only obstacle was the kingdom of Ndebele. Lobengula (ruled 1868–94), the Ndebele king, was tricked into signing away his kingdom but, in spite of blatant chicanery, the British government approved the treaty and Rhodes was free to colonise Zimbabwe, using his newly constituted company the British South Africa Company. A 'pioneer column' was dispatched to check out the abandoned Mutapa empire goldmines. There was little left, however; the ancients had done a thorough job. Nonetheless, the British launched an attack on Lobengula's capital Bulawayo which, with the help of the Maxim gun and cavalry, was successful. When Lobengula died in 1894, it seemed to mark the end for the Ndebele, but they rose up again in 1896, coming close to defeating their oppressors. The arrival of reinforcements from the Cape Colony eventually put a stop to any resistance.

The Second Boer War: 1899–1902

The Transvaal was operating more or less independently, but Britain remained responsible for the republic's foreign policy and 'native affairs'. The discovery of gold at Witwatersrand, however, changed everything. As the Transvaal government imposed heavy taxes on those engaged in mining the gold – mostly British – the British tried unsuccessfully to develop closer ties between the republic and the Cape Colony.

Eventually, as relationships deteriorated, the Boers became

increasingly convinced that the British government was trying to destroy Transvaal independence. This suspicion was encouraged by a madcap plan dreamed up by Cecil Rhodes, then Prime Minister of the Cape Colony, to send a British South Africa Company force into the Transvaal to overthrow the government by encouraging foreign workers to rebel. The initiative, known as the Jameson Raid from the name of its leader, Leander Starr Jameson (1853–1917), was an embarrassing failure that bred anti-British feeling not just in the Boer republics but also amongst the Afrikaners of the Cape Colony. Rhodes was forced to resign and the Transvaal and Orange Free State joined together in an alliance against Britain.

The danger now arose of the Transvaal allying itself with Germany and its goldmines possibly falling into the hands of Britain's greatest European rival. Britain argued with Transvaal president Paul Kruger (1825–1904) that foreign workers should be given the political rights so far denied them and that he should show favour to British mining interests. There was much sabre-rattling, and British troops were moved up to the Transvaal border. Kruger struck first, declaring war in October 1899, and sending his troops into the Cape Colony and Natal, this sudden mobilisation providing the Afrikaners with some early victories. But the British sent in a huge army of 500,000 men which captured the main Boer towns by the middle of 1900.

Kruger fled to Europe but commando raids persisted for another two years before the Boers were finally forced to surrender, mostly due to a ruthless 'scorched earth' strategy. Boer farms were destroyed by the British and the occupants were moved to concentration camps where more than 27,000 Boer women and children, and an unknown number of black Africans who were also interned, died. It was something Afrikaners would never forget and gave a strong impetus to the development of Afrikaner nationalism during subsequent decades.

Many black Africans had hoped that after the war – in which many of them had fought on the British side – the British would restore them to their land. They were to be disappointed when the British government launched a campaign to placate the Boers. It worked. In

1910, the former Boer republic of the Transvaal and the British colonies – Orange River (formerly the Boer republic Orange Free State), Natal and the Cape Colony – amalgamated in the Union of South Africa. With this, white domination of southern Africa was assured for decades to come.

Colonial Rule in Africa

For the next eighty years or so, colonial rule prevailed in Africa. It was a comparatively brief period in the continent's long history, but it changed everything forever. When the dust had settled on those eighty years, Africans had dispensed with their traditional modes of government and political systems. Although they had often regarded the European style of governance as an unnecessary imposition, one against which, within a few decades of the twentieth century, they had organised countless liberation movements, ironically they stuck with the systems with which they had been encumbered. The legacy of colonialism would, therefore, be strong, centralised, authoritarian governments – often dictatorships – and, after independence, the administration of many African nations remained little changed from that which had been imposed upon them. The administrations that were put in place to govern the new colonies had to be assembled very quickly because little thought had gone into what should happen after conquest or submission. Naturally, the officials who were put in place were Europeans who, in effect, made it up as they went along, although the traditions of law and government of the colonial power obviously had an influence on how things were done.

Of course, the lack of consideration of such matters can be ascribed to the rapaciousness of the various European powers. They saw no further than the resources and raw materials that were to be exploited and the new markets that were to be opened up. This was particularly the case with the concessionary companies that were often used to open up colonies. These were private companies, allocated vast areas of Africa to colonise at their own cost in the name of their country, an inexpensive option for the government concerned.

As we have already seen, Britain employed such companies as the Royal Niger Company, the British South Africa Company and the Imperial British East Africa Company and the Germans, French and Portuguese governments were no different. The intention was to open up the colony for exploitation, invest in infrastructure, such as railways and communications, and introduce a cash economy, an alien concept to the majority of Africans. In reality, little of the long-term investment actually happened and, in the desire for short-term gain for private individuals, abuse was rife. Many of the companies involved went bankrupt, leaving governments no option but to take over and rule directly.

This meant the appointment of colonial administrators, each of whom knew that his fiefdom had to be economically self-sufficient, that he could not look to the taxpayer in the home country to pick up the tab for his government's imperial aspirations. Administrations, therefore, had to be run on a shoestring but they were also expected to deliver revenue. Africans played no more than junior roles in these administrations, employed as clerks, typists and policemen and working long hours for low wages. Europeans held the high-ranking political and administrative positions, as well as senior military ranks.

It soon became evident that nineteenth century optimism about Africa's untapped resources was misplaced. This was emphasised by the collapse of the trade in wild rubber around 1910, rubber by then being produced much more economically on plantations in Southeast Asia. The only safe bet for outside investment was the mining of gold, copper and diamonds. White settlement, attempted in almost every colony, was strenuously opposed by Africans. In a number of regions – Gold Coast, southern Nigeria and Bechuanaland, for example – they successfully campaigned to keep white farmers out.

In Algeria, white settlers grabbed most of the arable land, leaving the Muslims whose land they had stolen only the poorer land to work. This resulted in deterioration of the land and famine. Muslim farmers were also punitively taxed which forced them to work for low wages on the farms owned by the white settlers who were the ones to benefit from the tax paid by those same workers. It was a template that was followed in Kenya and Rhodesia but life was made more complicated for the black farmer in Kenya by a pass system that restricted movement outside the 'reserves' that had been established. Again, money was ploughed into helping white settlers, via subsidies and marketing assistance. Further resentment on the part of black farmers arose from the fact that not much more than 10 per cent of white settlers' land in Kenya and Rhodesia was given over to agriculture whereas they had to work on land in their overcrowded 'reserves'.

In terms of crops, groundnuts were the main cash crop of Nigeria and Senegal; coffee was produced successfully in Cote d'Ivoire, Angola, Tanganyika, Uganda and eastern Belgian Congo; and cocoa was the main crop of Gold Coast and south-western Nigeria. Against the wishes of the colonial powers, no one wanted to grow cotton. It was labour-intensive and did not bring great financial reward. It was produced only under threat as in the case of French-controlled Ubangui-Chari (modern-day Central African Republic), Upper Volta (modern-day Burkina Faso), French Sudan (modern-day Mali) and Niger, in which cases it was grown to supply the French textile industry.

There was still a great deal of rural poverty, despite the success of cash-crop production, and African industrial self-sufficiency was undermined by the importation of mass-produced European cloth and metal goods. They were undercut on price on items such as rice, imported from French Indo-China and sold cheaper than locally produced rice. Furthermore, the large European companies at the coast made sure that African producers received the lowest possible price for the goods they produced for export while price increases for imported goods were immediately passed on to African buyers.

A head-tax on all adult men, levied by many colonial authorities, also served to disrupt African rural self-sufficiency, forcing everyone into the cash economy. This often meant that men had to migrate to places where they could earn wages, far from their own land. Their families were left behind trying to grow enough food to feed themselves. Even when the migrant returned home, however, he rarely had enough to pay his taxes as well as properly feed his family.

Agents were sent out from all the centres of European industry to recruit large numbers of unskilled workers and the monopolies given to recruitment agencies meant that very low wages could be offered. Workers had no other option but to accept them if they wanted to work. In effect, it was still slavery.

Christianity in Colonial Africa

When the European powers dismantled African political authority, they were also diminishing the authority of traditional African religion, vested as it often was in the chief, the guardian of the ancestral spirits and the shrines at which they were worshipped. This presented a major opportunity for Christian missionaries to fill the spiritual void. In the first few decades of the twentieth century, therefore, there was a flood of new believers. There was often a pragmatic element to many of these 'conversions'. Missions provided a degree of education as well as some health provision through medical clinics. Naturally, the new colonial administrations paid little heed to the provision of such services. The missions, consequently, began to attract thousands of people who saw a way of improving their lot or just ensuring that they and their families were kept free of disease.

In southern Africa in the 1880s and 1890s, however, the 'Ethiopian Church' movement – from the word used in the Bible for 'Africa' – was launched. A number of African clergymen broke away from European churches to establish their own independent churches. The movement spread northwards to central Africa. African clergymen in these new churches took the Bible at face value, believing the literal nature of its content. The 'second coming' was, consequently, taken by them to mean the sweeping away of colonial oppression, lending a nationalist motivation to their teachings, perhaps one of the earliest expressions of such sentiments in Africa. Significant names in the movement were Nyasaland-born Elliot Kanan Kamwana (c. 1882–1956), founder of the Watch Tower movement, and Nyasaland rebel preacher John Chilembwe (1871–1915).

States under Colonial Rule

King Leopold declared that all unoccupied and uncultivated land in his new, personal colony of Congo Free State belonged to him. This, of course, meant virtually everywhere as the sparsely populated forest was largely unoccupied. Most of the land was subsequently leased to private companies which were ruthless in their collection of rubber to satisfy the huge European demand. Failure to meet rubber collection quotas was punishable by death, the *Force Publique* required to provide the hands of its victims as proof that they had killed them. Villages would often attack each other in order to collect hands as insurance against failure to achieve impossible quotas and the *Force Publique* were paid their bonuses according to the number of severed hands they presented. This grotesque situation is summed up by Peter Forbath in his book *The River Congo: The Discovery, Exploration and Exploitation of the World's Most Dramatic River* (Harper & Row, New York, 1977):

'The baskets of severed hands, set down at the feet of the European post commanders, became the symbol of the Congo Free State... The collection of hands became an end in itself. *Force Publique* soldiers brought them to the stations in place of rubber; they even went out to harvest them instead of rubber... They became a sort of currency. They came to be used to make up for shortfalls in rubber quotas, to replace... the people who were demanded for the forced labour gangs; and the *Force Publique* soldiers were paid their bonuses on the basis of how many hands they collected.'

Many Congolese obtained firearms and began to use them against the state and, by the early years of the twentieth century, armed rebellion was frequent. Word spread of the atrocities and there was international condemnation. This, coupled with the collapse in the world price of rubber, persuaded Leopold to hand over his African colony to the Belgian government in 1908. The worst of the abuses were ended, even though private companies still exploited the region's resources. However, up to eight million of the estimated sixteen million inhabitants of the Congo Free State died between 1885 and 1908, as a result of warfare, starvation, disease and state murder.

In West Africa, raw material production was left largely in the hands of African peasant farmers, willing workers compared to the forced labour that had to be used by European farmers. Their colonial masters forced them away from the production of food crops towards cash crops suited to European markets. Production was stimulated, however, by the improvement of the infrastructure. New railways, such as the one from Dakar to Bamako, facilitated the transport of materials, of which groundnuts and palm oil, staple export crops prior to colonisation, remained important after it. Africans themselves showed initiative, however. Tetteh Quarshie (1842–92), from the Gold Coast, was selling cocoa seeds to local farmers by the 1890s. Cultivation of cocoa spread and, by 1914, the Gold Coast was the world's largest producer of cocoa. A railway built by the British from Lagos to Ibadan and Kano in modern-day Nigeria helped cocoa to prosper in the territories of the Yoruba. And the Hausa began successfully to produce groundnuts but not the much riskier and less lucrative cotton that the British had urged them to produce. Of course, these railways, roads and harbours had to be paid for somehow, although certainly not by the domestic taxpayer of the colonial power. Neither did the European traders and manufacturers who made fortunes from the improved transport network cough up. Instead, Africans paid through taxation and customs duties on imports.

In East Africa, persuading African farmers to grow cotton was also a problem. There was more money to be had from other crops such as groundnuts or palm oil. Only in Egypt and Uganda did the British Cotton Growing Association meet with any success. After they had established a protectorate over Uganda, the British had come to an arrangement with the Christian aristocracy of the kingdom of Buganda, one of the colony's many kingdoms. They promised that, rather than encourage white settlement of the region, they would institute a system of private land tenure with the nobility as the landlords and the peasants as tenants. With this, they succeeded in removing the single most important tenet of the authority of the *kabaka*, reducing him to little more than a figurehead whose appointment was the prerogative of colonial administrators. It was a system that was introduced in the other kingdoms. In return, however, a new railway from the Indian Ocean port of Mombasa, on the coast of the East African Protectorate, to Kisumo on Lake Victoria Nyanza gave the Baganda access to the coast. It was used to transport the cotton that was grown in Uganda in increasing quantities, mostly through the efforts of the chiefs who distributed the seeds to peasant farmers. The excellent climate and soil of Uganda made agriculture a great success and its people enjoyed a greater degree of security of food supply than anywhere else on the African continent at the time.

The temperate climate and fertile soils of the highlands that lay to the east of Lake Victoria Nyanza meant that the East African Protectorate – re-named Kenya in 1920 – was earmarked for white settlement by the British from the start. Furthermore, the Uganda railway, which advertised the highlands of British East Africa as a 'Winter Home for Aristocrats', ran through the region. Nonetheless, the people on whose land the whites wanted to settle – the highlands were allocated for white settlement only – fought hard to retain it, with a series of wars between 1901 and 1908. A violent response by British military forces eventually brought this resistance to a bloody close. Meanwhile, white settlers were brought in from Britain and South Africa in large numbers and they took an active role in the colony's administration.

The colonising of German East Africa (modern-day Tanzania) had been hard going for the Germans but seemed to have been accomplished by the late 1890s, although they had a fairly weak grip on the colony, only exerting control through a series of forts. A head tax imposed in 1898 created resentment and often could only be collected using violence. The governor ordered villages to grow cotton, taking villagers away from their other work and affecting the social fabric of the country, as women were forced to stand in for the absent men. The resentment finally erupted in 1905 when an uprising broke out in the south of the colony. As drought ravaged the region, the people of the Matumbi Hills refused to grow cotton. Violence ensued and attacks on foreigners spread across the region. The rebels turned to spiritual inspiration to defeat the colonists, sprinkling their bodies with 'war medicine' called *maji* that was said to turn bullets into water. The uprising became known as the '*Maji Maji* Rebellion'. After initial successes, probably due to the Germans' lack of readiness, the rebels were shocked when thousands of them were mown down by a machine gun post in one action. *Maji-maji* did not possess the powers they thought it did. The Germans brought in reinforcements and, in 1906, the region was brought back under control. The German 'scorched earth' policy brought famine to southern and central parts of the territory in which up to 50,000 people died. The uprising had taught the German colonials a lesson, however, and they reduced the level of violence with which they ruled German East Africa. However, the local people had also learned from events and their sacrifice would later inspire those involved in the struggle for independence.

In the highlands of German South West Africa, the Germans pursued white settlement to the detriment of Nama and Herero pastoralists, already reeling from an epidemic of rinderpest amongst their cattle in 1896–97. The Herero rebelled in 1904, reoccupying their territory and killing around a hundred Germans, but they were trapped after the Germans brought in reinforcements. At this point, the German general, Lothar von Trotha (1848–1920), issued a chilling ultimatum to the Herero:

'The Hereros are German subjects no longer. They have killed, stolen, cut off the ears and other parts of the body of wounded soldiers, and now are too cowardly to want to fight any longer... The Herero nation must now leave the country. If it refuses, I shall compel it to do so with the 'long tube' (cannon). Any Herero found inside the German frontier, with or without a gun or cattle, will be executed. I shall spare neither women nor children. I shall give the order to drive them away and fire on them.'

(*Absolute Destruction: Military Culture and the Practices of War in Imperial Germany*, Isabel V. Hull, Cornell University Press, New York, 2006)

The Herero were driven westwards into the Kalahari Desert where many died of hunger and lack of water. Hereros who survived were herded into camps and used as forced labour. By 1905, only 15,000 survived of a 1904 population of 80,000. Von Trotha used the same tactics on the Nama, who had also risen up. Around 10,000 perished, and the 9,000 survivors were confined to concentration camps. With their chiefs deposed and their cattle taken from them, the Herero and the Nama served as a low-paid workforce in German farms and mines. Their hatred for their colonial overlords remained intense.

Africa and the First World War

The outbreak of the First World War in 1914 had implications for Africa, even though the main fighting was taking place thousands of miles to the north. Britain overran Germany's West African colonies, Togo and Kamerun, which had only recently been acquired and were poorly defended. South African troops had, meanwhile, occupied German South West Africa. The conflict in East Africa lasted until November 1917, by which time British troops had occupied it from the north and Belgians from the west. However, the German commander, Lieutenant Colonel Paul Emil von Lettow-Vorbeck (1870–1964), led his troops into Portuguese East Africa, waging a victorious campaign through Mozambique, Nyasaland and north-eastern Rhodesia.

The war was costly to Africans. A million of them served as porters in the various armies and around 100,000 died of disease, hunger or overwork. The destruction was huge. Villages and towns were destroyed and food supplies were requisitioned by troops of both sides, leaving people to endure terrible hardship. The troops engaged in the fighting were, largely, African. The British recruited from Sierra Leone, Gold Coast and Nigeria for the campaign in East Africa while the Germans recruited their *askaris* – Swahili for 'soldiers' – from recently-conquered tribes. Meanwhile, the South Africans did not permit their black recruits to carry rifles. Around 150,000 West Africans fought for the French in Europe, of whom around 30,000 were killed in action.

The influenza epidemic that ravaged the entire world in 1918–19, immediately after the war, devastated Africa, causing havoc amongst people already weakened by famine, hunger and desperate working conditions. Some parts of the continent lost up to 3 per cent of their population. The European powers occupying German colonies at the end of the war took control of them. France and Britain shared Kamerun, Belgium took over Rwanda and Burundi, Britain kept Tanganyika and South Africa was allowed to hang on to German South West Africa. The regions were held by these powers under League of Nations mandates, but they were treated, effectively, as colonies.

The Inter-War Years

The years between the wars marked the high-water mark of colonial rule in Africa. Although Africans had little say in the government of their countries, there was a definite change in attitude. 'Lessons of experience' had been learned from the early days of colonialism, resulting in more efficient and uniform types of administration. Thankfully, following the exposure of previous scandalous behaviour, the more abhorrent abuses and exploitation diminished. This, however, did not make for much of an improvement in the lives of ordinary Africans.

European administrators were frequently forced to turn to surviving African leaders to help them execute colonial policy, often resorting to bribery and flattery to gain their support. If this help was not forthcoming, a malleable official would be appointed to a position of importance who would readily carry out the wishes of the administrator. This was a system enthusiastically embraced by the British – although used to some extent by every colonial power – and designated as 'Indirect Rule' or ruling through what they termed 'Native Authorities'. Africans were encouraged to develop in an 'African' way, by making Hausa or Swahili the language of government, by ensuring rigid social segregation between Africans and Europeans and by establishing limits to European immigration. Chiefs were permitted by the British to mediate in local civil disputes and even to preside over some criminal cases but they were barred from serious criminal cases or any in which a European was involved. Their employment in this way was of great benefit to the colonial authority because it saved money. It also created a perception of local involvement in administrative duties.

It is understandable, however, that traditional leaders might not have wanted to carry out some of the duties required of them in the 'Indirect Rule' system as they were often unpopular initiatives that rapidly led to resentment and dissent. They included duties such as the recruitment of troops for the colonial army, tax collection and sourcing labour for public works or for agricultural work on farms owned by Europeans. Furthermore, the belief still lingered in the minds of the European administrators that Africans and African culture were inferior to their European equivalents. So, at the same time as they were encouraging Africans to develop their institutions in an African way, the Europeans persisted in imposing upon them Western styles and techniques of government. Or they simply adapted or even invented local 'customary law' to suit them.

In Africa before the Europeans arrived there had been a great deal of overlap between societies, in terms of language and custom. The British, however, basing their entire administrative system on what they perceived to be a series of separate chiefdoms, emphasised the differences in dress, construction techniques and religion, creating rigid 'tribal' distinctions. 'Tribe' was used pejoratively, to confirm the perceived backwardness of African societies. Of course, this emphasis on the differences between peoples also served to prevent them from uniting against the colonial power. In Southern Rhodesia, for example, groups or 'tribes' lived in 'reserves', kept apart from each other.

To enable African administrators to function in the language of their relevant colonial power, of course, they had to be educated. Western-style education was made available but was often restricted. In the Congo, for instance, the Belgian authorities provided a good education to high school level, but Africans were prohibited from going to university. There were various styles and theories of administration, although there was much that they had in common with each other. The French initially espoused the policy of assimilation which grew out of the French Revolution and, especially, the 1789 *Declaration of the Rights of Man and of the Citizen* that stated that all men are born free and have equal rights. This meant, therefore, that those born in the colonies shared those rights. France attempted to assimilate its colonial citizens by imbuing them with French language and culture. This, although apparently less overtly racist than 'Indirect Rule', implied, nonetheless, that French culture was inherently superior to that of Africa. Within a couple of decades of the beginning of colonial rule, it became evident that France's colonial subjects were not suddenly going to become French and a policy of 'association' was introduced which was 'Indirect Rule' by another name. It was possible for a French colonial subject to become a French citizen with all the rights of someone born in Paris and the Portuguese also made this offer available, but it was permitted only for a tiny percentage of the colonial population. Similarly, British-trained professionals, such as doctors or lawyers, could become British citizens.

Eventually, private companies began to disappear from colonies and the colonial powers took over, borrowing and sharing ideas, ultimately developing administrations that resembled each other. Most colonies were broken down into districts, governed by a District Commissioner, a Commissioner or a *Commandant de Cercle*, his responsibilities including everything from judicial appeals to taxation. He also decided on matters such as road-building and education, bringing in specialists for most departments. The next administrative level, in the larger colonies at any rate, was the province which grouped several districts together. Above this structure was the governor who normally ruled through an administrative council, an advisory cabinet that was often made up of the heads of the various departments and sometimes included a few traditional rulers.

However, there was a considerable degree of stability in the African colonies between the wars, mainly because the colonial administrations took little notice of African views inside government. Opposition was mostly expressed through riots, civil disobedience, religious movements and farmers' protests. But, by the end of the thirties, the pressure for reform in Africa was beginning to emerge from Europe itself. The Second World War would intervene, however, making reform less of a priority to embattled Europeans.

South Africa

South Africa was unique in being the only place on the continent where the settler community actually became dominant over the African majority and managed to wrest independence from the European colonial power, in this case the British. After the Second Boer War, the Boers of the Transvaal elected as Prime Minister Louis Botha (1862–1919) who had been commander-in-chief of the Transvaal Boers in the Second Boer War and, as his deputy, Jan Smuts (1870–1950) who had also fought in that conflict. South African unification, merging the British colonies of Natal and Cape Colony with the former Boer republics of Transvaal and the Orange Free State, was an inevitability but it took some negotiation to bring it about. Finally, in 1910, the Union of South Africa was born. Only 'European' men could stand for election to Parliament and the same rule applied to voting, in any province but the Cape. The historic divisions between the Afrikaner and the British South African constituted the country's main political division, each pursuing his own vested interests. In the middle were parties that were a mixture of British and Boer. The British, however, never won a majority in Parliament.

Smuts and Botha belonged to the South Africa Party, the objective of which was to blur the differences between the two nationalities and to cooperate with the British government. They remained in power until 1924 when the National Party, led by J.B.M. Hertzog (1866–1942), pursuing economic nationalism and separation from British influence, formed a coalition with the Labour Party and ruled for the next nine years. In 1933, in the shadow of the Depression, the National and South Africa parties came together to create the United Party. Finally, in 1948, a more radically racist National Party was elected to govern. It would hold office until 1994. The National Party initiated the first moves towards *apartheid* – separation – for the races. It first tried to achieve this on a geographic basis, the African majority being housed in 'reserves', euphemistically called 'homelands'.

After 1910, like Canada, New Zealand and Australia, South Africa became increasingly self-governing and then, in 1931, with the Statute of Westminster, the British government gave it legal independence. In 1961, after many years of agitation by Afrikaner republicans, South Africa voted to become a republic. At the same time, in the midst of fierce criticism by member states of its racial policies, it withdrew from membership of the Commonwealth. Voting rights for Africans and 'Coloured' people of the Cape Province were negligible throughout these years. In 1936, Africans were given the right to elect three Europeans to represent them in Parliament, and in 1957 'Coloured' voters were permitted to elect four Europeans. Both these initiatives were abolished in the 1960s, however. From then until 1994, only Europeans were permitted to vote.

The lack of voting rights did not deter Africans from political activism, however. The African National Congress (ANC) was founded in 1912, the South African Indian Congress in 1920 and the African Political Organisation (APO) was founded by Dr. Abdullah Abdurahman (1872–1940) to represent 'Coloured' people in 1902. Initially, these organisations remained peaceful pressure groups aimed at gradual enfranchisement of all classes, colours and sexes. The ANC was led by lawyers, clergymen and journalists who wanted to redress the injustices of the system by constitutional means. By 1948, however, having protested against every single piece of racist legislation, it had become apparent that lobbying, sending delegations overseas and protesting peacefully were achieving little.

Meanwhile, South Africa had gained control over German South West Africa during the First World War under a League of Nations mandate. However, when, after the Second World War, the other countries handed their mandated territories over to the United Nations in preparation for independence, South Africa refused. Namibia remained under South African control until 1988, when the government finally acceded to international pressure.

The Second World War

Africans had to endure many of the same privations suffered by Europeans during the Second World War and their young men were conscripted to fight, many of them never returning home. This conflict, however, was of far greater significance to Africa than the Great War, leading, as it did, to the eventual collapse of colonial rule.

In effect, the war began earlier in Africa than in Europe where Germany's invasion of Poland, in September 1939, was the catalyst for the conflict. In May 1936, the Italian dictator Benito Mussolini (1883–1945) invaded Ethiopia with a huge force of 120,000 soldiers and 300 tanks. By the end of the campaign, Mussolini had deployed more than 400,000 African and Italian troops in the conquest of Ethiopia. Emperor Haile Selassie (1892–1975) fled into exile in England where he remained for five years, leading a government-in-exile and trying to secure foreign help. In 1940, the Italian forces in Ethiopia, Somalia and Eritrea became cut off by British, Indian and African armies in Kenya and the Sudan when Italy entered the war on the side of the Germans. They were easily defeated, allowing the emperor to return in 1941.

Although Africans fought in the Second World War, the continent's most significant role was in the provision of raw materials, especially after the fall of Southeast Asia to the Japanese. Africans were exhorted to produce more groundnuts and cotton and the continent became the Allies' only source of palm oil. Forced labour helped to keep tin production up in the tin mines of Nigeria and, once Malaya had fallen, wild rubber from the forests of the Zaire Basin again became essential. Meanwhile, all across British Africa, villages were ordered to produce extra food supplies for the war effort.

Another effect of war was the improvement of the infrastructure in a number of places. Harbours were deepened and airports constructed. Many Africans moved into urban centres seeking work on these installations or fleeing unachievable demands for extra crops in the countryside. In South Africa, the steel industry received a boost from the need for repairs to Allied shipping and manufacturing overtook mining as the principal employer and source of revenue for the country. Black South Africans were responding to the grinding poverty they were experiencing in the countryside and to further land restrictions by flooding into the urban centres of Witwatersrand, Cape Town and Port Elizabeth. For some, it was a good move, but for many, unable to find a job, it was a case of replacing one kind of poverty with another. The return from the war of the 200,000 white troops and 100,000 black troops only served to exacerbate the situation.

In the war itself, the biggest direct impact was felt through the North African Campaign which lasted for three years and was fought in the Libyan and Egyptian deserts as well as in Morocco, Algeria and Tunisia. By May 1943, the Allies' control of North Africa was won and, from there, the invasion of Sicily and Italy was launched.

The Second World War sounded the death-knell for colonialism in Africa. Forced cropping had increased Africans' hatred for the colonial powers and returning servicemen brought back a heightened awareness of the wider world. Africans also realised, at last, that the colonial powers were not invincible and that change was possible. On the other hand, Europeans, especially the French, felt indebted to Africa for its war effort. Furthermore, to obtain the support of Africans, Europeans had promised reform when victory came. In British Africa, educated Africans even began to fill senior positions in the administrations and President Charles de Gaulle (1890–1970) of

France promised a 'new deal' for French colonial subjects. When, in the years immediately after the war, India, Pakistan and Sri Lanka threw off the colonial yoke, momentum for similar treatment for African peoples began to build.

Nationalism and Independence

The Struggle for Freedom

Apart from the rise of independent churches preaching the overthrow of the colonial powers, there were numerous instances of overt opposition. In the late 1920s, for instance, 350,000 Gbaya in French Equatorial Africa revolted. Needless to say, the rebellion was ruthlessly suppressed in yet another colonial atrocity. At the same time, although trade unions had been made illegal for Africans, they still succeeded in mounting a number of strikes in pursuit of better pay and conditions, such as the ones in the mines and railways of Guinea, Sierra Leone and Gold Coast in the 1920s. Others followed in Northern Rhodesia's Copperbelt in 1935 and 1940. These gave Africans hope and the realisation that, with a united front, change was possible. Across the continent, welfare organisations were springing up, protesting against instances of local injustice. Inevitably, too, the new and increasing educated elite, those who had been trained to work within the administrations or to be teachers or clergymen, were beginning to question the way that Africans were being treated. Their exclusion from the politics of their own countries gave rise to growing anger. They were still a long way, however, from considering political independence as the solution.

The Pan-African movement emerged in the United States and the Caribbean during the 1920s, its genesis credited to the Trinidadian lawyer and writer Henry Sylvester Williams (1869–1911) who stated that 'the time has come when the voice of Black men should be heard independently in their own affairs'. Pan-Africanism sought to unite all Africans into one 'African community'. The most significant advocate of Pan-Africanism was Jamaican-born publisher, journalist and orator Marcus Garvey (1887–1940), who promoted the return to their African homelands of slaves and their descendants. To this end, he founded the shipping company Black Star Line to effect the transportation. Garvey never actually visited Africa but founded the Universal Negro Improvement Association and published a very successful newspaper called *The Negro World*. His message of 'Africa for the Africans' served as an inspiration for many of the young men and women who would take part in the nationalist movements in the 1940s and 1950s. Meanwhile, the francophone movement Négritude was launched in France in the 1930s by a group of writers who celebrated their common black identity and the ancient cultures of Africa. It symbolised an outright rejection of the French ideology of 'assimilation'.

The only place on the African continent where a nationalist movement actually achieved its objectives between the wars was Egypt, which had suffered hardships during the First World War as the British demanded food, animals and labour. Britain had declared a Protectorate over the country in 1914, replacing the *khedive* ('viceroy') with a relative who was appointed Sultan. In 1919, a delegation of the nationalist Wafd party, including its leader Saad Zaghloul (1895–1927), attended the Paris Peace Conference to demand independence for Egypt. They were arrested and deported to Malta, leading to huge demonstrations by both Christians and Muslims in Egypt during which 800 people lost their lives. Eventually, in 1922, agreement was reached to give Egypt independence with parliamentary government and Sultan Fuad (ruled 1922–1936) as king. The British, however, remained in occupation and continued to be the real power in the country. In the 1930s, a new Islamist group, the Muslim Brotherhood, began to agitate against European influence and corruption at the highest levels of government, introducing young Egyptians to Islamic nationalism. It soon began to spread to other countries.

Post-War Development and Investment

Although little was set to change in colonies under Belgian or Portuguese control after the Second World War, there was little doubt that the British and the French had seen during the conflict just how valuable their African colonies could be. Therefore, they both established investment funds through the British Colonial Development and Welfare Acts of 1940 and 1945 and the French *Fonds d'Investissements pour le Developpement Economique et Social* of 1946. Unfortunately, however, much of this investment was diverted to industries that were in the hands of Europeans such as mining in the Gold Coast and Nigeria and white settler farming in Kenya and Southern Rhodesia. Rural Africa, home to the majority of Africans, received none of it.

Nothing had really changed. The colonial powers still perceived Africa as a supplier of raw materials and an importer of European manufactured goods. Certainly, there was a boom in the 1950s as Europe snapped up African minerals and agricultural raw materials but it was in no way a result of investment by the colonial powers. One area, however, where British investment did make a difference was social welfare, often after demands by increasingly vocal nationalists. New hospitals were built and universities were opened in order to satisfy the demand for civil servants and teachers. The French, in accordance with their philosophy of assimilation, simply presumed anyone wanting a university education would seek it in France.

Both Britain and France seemed to be resigned to eventual independence for their African colonies but they wanted it to happen according to their timetable and that meant gradually. It was not to be, however. The rapid growth of nationalism was the critical factor and, by the early 1960s, almost every African colony had achieved political, if not economic independence. It did not come without a degree of pain – a considerable amount in some places – especially those with a large population of white settlers. Therefore, whereas West African states with little white settlement proceeded to independence without too much trouble, others, such as Algeria, Kenya and

Southern Rhodesia erupted into conflict, the white settlers themselves intervening to prevent self-determination.

Independence

West Africa

Gold Coast, a country of around five million people, was in the vanguard of independence. The British had already ensured an African majority on the Gold Coast Legislative Council in 1946, although these representatives were appointed by the country's chiefs and still fell within the Indirect Rule system the British employed in most of its African colonies. In 1947, the United Gold Coast Convention (UGCC) was founded by prominent businessmen and lawyers with the objective of increasing the number of elected members of the government. Kwame Nkrumah (1909–72), a former teacher who had been inspired by the Pan-Africanist teachings of Marcus Garvey, was its leader. In 1948, in Accra, police opened fire on a demonstration of ex-servicemen protesting about the rising cost of living. Rioting broke out in other Gold Coast towns and Nkrumah and other UGCC leaders were arrested.

Although the British increased African representation on the Legislative Council, it was not enough for Nkrumah, who had founded the Convention People's Party (CPP), demanding 'self-government now'. In the 1951 election, after the CPP won a majority, Nkrumah was released from prison to form a government as 'leader of government business' but there was still an overwhelming number of members of the government who were nominated by the chiefs. After three years of negotiation, however, the country was finally granted fully-elected self-government. Nkrumah's party won the subsequent election and he became its first prime minister.

In March 1957, Gold Coast became independent, taking the name 'Ghana' but it was evident from the start that all was not going to be plain sailing. The Ashanti cocoa farmers resented the fact that the government still brought in large profits from its marketing boards but persisted in imposing restricted prices on them. This led to the founding of the National Liberation Movement in Ashanti. Nonetheless, the independence of Ghana, the first African state to achieve it, was a shining beacon to African nationalists across the continent, one they hoped soon to follow. And, indeed, Ghana's example was rapidly followed in the next few years by many of Britain's African colonies.

Nigeria was an entirely different proposition to Ghana. A large and disunited territory of 35 million people, there were regional splits within it and the country had been governed as two entirely separate territories until 1946. The nationalist lead in Nigeria was taken by the National Council of Nigeria and Cameroons (NCNC) which was founded in 1944 and numbered amongst its founders Nnamdi Azikiwe (1904–96), editor of the newspaper the *West African Pilot*, which he used to promote Nigerian nationalism. The main support for the NCNC lay in the south-eastern Igbo country, but it was Azikiwe's intention to make his group national. Other regionally-based parties were formed, however, and they could not agree on a constitution, delaying independence. Eventually, the problems resolved, Nigeria gained its independence in October 1960 with the northern Nigerian Sir Abubakar Tafawa Balewa (1912–66) as its first prime minister. Tensions were already evident, however, and regional conflict and civil war were inevitable.

In Sierra Leone, too, regional divides played their part in the independence struggle. The Mende peoples of the interior triumphed over the Freetown Creoles who had formerly been dominant in the country. Independence was granted in April 1961 and Sir Milton Margai (1895–1964) was sworn in as prime minister. The years following independence were prosperous as Sierra Leone enjoyed the revenue from its mineral resources. The tiny neighbouring state of The Gambia, meanwhile, fought off plans for its union with its neighbour Senegal and became independent in 1965.

In French West and Equatorial Africa, nationalists were prepared to accept the French approach to independence – the pace of reform would be dictated by France and the African colonies would remain within 'Greater France'. In return, however, they expected to enjoy the rights of full French citizens. It was soon evident that this was not going to be the case. They were permitted, for example, only ten delegates to the French National Assembly, a number vastly disproportionate to the number of people they were expected to represent.

There were differences of opinion amongst the various groupings of African nationalists about what would be the best approach to take in their negotiations with France about independence. Senegalese nationalist and poet Léopold Senghor (1906–2001) was leader of the *Bloc Démocratique Senegalais* in the National Assembly, supporting a federal approach, along with Niger, Chad, and French Sudan (Mali). The French West African territories would form one federation while French Equatorial Africa would form another. Meanwhile, Félix Houphouët-Boigny (1905–93), leader of the *Rassemblement Démocratique Africain* (RDA), who would become the first President of Côte d'Ivoire, opposed federation as he feared that, in such a set-up, his country's wealth from its lucrative coffee, palm oil and cocoa exports would be used to prop up the other, poorer nations. The French tried to satisfy some of the demands of the nationalists to prevent a situation arising like the one they had experienced in Algeria where, since 1954, they had been engaged in a war of liberation with nationalists. By 1956, each territory in the region was granted fully-elected, internal self-government, although France still controlled defence, foreign policy and the economy.

When he was elected French President in 1958, Charles de Gaulle was determined to dispense with his country's increasing problems in Africa. He announced a referendum to take place in September 1958 to give the peoples of the French colonies the chance to express whether they wished to maintain the link with France or to be granted complete independence. Remarkably, the only state to vote '*Non*' was Guinea which became independent under President Ahmed Seoul Touré (1922–84) a month after the referendum. France immediately took revenge by withdrawing all its officials from Guinea in an attempt to demonstrate to its other colonial territories just how much they relied on the mother country. The remainder voted to remain with France in the belief that there would be more reforms but, when these were not forthcoming, they were soon demanding independence. In one remarkable year, 1960, known as the 'Year of Africa', thirteen French colonies – Mauritania, the Mali Federation, Gabon, the Republic of Congo (Brazzaville), the Central African Republic, Chad, Côte d'Ivoire, Niger, Upper Volta (later Burkina Faso), Dahomey (later Benin), Madagascar, Togo and Cameroon, finally gained their independence.

North Africa

After the Second World War, Sultan Mohammad V (ruled 1927–61) of Morocco antagonised the French, who had been ruling his country as a Protectorate, by supporting the Muslim nationalist movement, the Istiqlal (Independence) Party. Moroccan nationalists, like many in Africa, were disappointed when Allied victory failed to deliver independence. The French refused even to introduce reforms and tension grew. Eventually, in 1953, the sultan was forced into exile in Madagascar by the French. But, instead of disappearing from view, he became a national hero and a symbol of the independence struggle. Violence in the country increased until the French, already mired in the independence war in Algeria, eventually conceded defeat. Mohammad V was brought back and independence was granted in 1956. At the same time, Tunisia also became independent, under the presidency of Habib Bourguiba (1903–2000).

Algeria was France's most important colony in North Africa and she was determined to hold on to it to protect the two million French settlers living there. The struggle was a bloody one. It began in May 1945 when a nationalist demonstration erupted into a riot as a result of which around a hundred Europeans and thousands of Muslims were killed. However, the real war began on 1 November 1954 when the *Front de Liberation Nationale* (FLN) launched attacks throughout Algeria. The French, quickly realising the scale of the struggle, poured many thousands of troops into the country until, by 1958, they numbered 500,000. It turned into a long, bitterly fought war in which thousands of French soldiers and hundreds of thousands of Algerians lost their lives. Eventually, by 1962, the French had endured enough and independence was granted under the leadership of President Ahmed Ben Bella (b. 1918).

Meanwhile, in 1949, the United Nations General Assembly passed a resolution declaring that Libya, under British occupation since 1943, should be granted independence. On Christmas Eve, 1951, King Idris I (ruled 1951–69) proclaimed the United Kingdom of Libya. He was Libya's first and only king as he was ousted in 1969 by a military coup led by Colonel Mu'ammar al-Qadhdhafi (known as Gaddafi) (1942–2011) who pursued a radical Muslim revolution in the country until he was ousted in 2011.

Egypt, Sudan, Eritrea and Somalia

King Farouk (ruled 1936–1952) came to the throne in 1936 but, by 1952, Egyptians were tired of his corrupt and oppressive rule, and ashamed of the humiliating defeat inflicted on the Egyptian army by Israel in 1948–49. Eventually, in that year, he was deposed by a military coup. By 1954, Colonel Gamal 'Abd al-Nasir (known in English as Nasser) (1918–1970) had emerged as leader of the ruling military council and, in 1956, he became President of Egypt. One of his first acts was to nationalise the Suez Canal. Britain and France responded by invading Egypt to occupy the Canal Zone but overwhelming international opposition to their action, especially from the United States and the Soviet Union, and stubborn Egyptian resistance, forced them humiliatingly to withdraw their troops. In revenge, Nasser nationalised all French and British companies in Egypt, marking the end of more than a century of European domination in the country.

Following Egypt's renunciation of its historic claim on the Sudan in 1954, Britain granted hasty independence to the Sudanese. With the north of the country being Muslim, however, and the south non-Muslim, internal unity became a huge problem. Sudan was devastated by civil war during the 1960s that would also break out in the 1980s and 1990s. Ethiopia was keen to gain access to the sea and saw Eritrea as the means of doing so. Britain, eager to maintain Christian Ethiopia as a bulwark against increasing Muslim power in

Egypt and Arabia, allowed Emperor Haile Selassie to take over Eritrea in 1952 as a self-governing state in an Ethiopian federation. In 1962, however, Ethiopia annexed Eritrea leading to an armed struggle by liberation movements. Only in 1993 did Eritrea finally gain independence. British and Italian Somaliland gained independence in 1960, immediately merging to create the republic of Somalia.

British East Africa

In 1951, thousands of Meru farmers in Tanganyika were evicted from their land in order to allow a few white settlers to farm there. Mass protests persuaded former teacher Julius Nyerere (1922–1999), to form the political party, the Tanganyika African National Union (TANU). Following the example of Nkrumah's CPP in Ghana, he succeeded in turning his party into a national force while the British attempted to create what they termed a 'multi-racial' constitution. In reality, this was a means of giving the European and Asian minority the biggest say in governing the country. But Nyerere persuaded a number of white settler politicians onto his side and TANU won the 1958 general election. Tanganyika was granted independence in December 1961 and, in 1964, amalgamated with Zanzibar to create the United Republic of Tanzania. It was only a matter of time before the other nations of British East Africa followed suit.

In Tanganyika, political unity had been facilitated to some extent by a common language, Swahili, which helped to make Tanganyikans feel that they were part of the same country. In Uganda, however, there was no such national unity. Buganda had always occupied a special position, ruled separately within the British Protectorate of Uganda. The Kabaka, Mutesa II (ruled 1939–1969), was determined to retain his province's special status and, indeed, in the 1961 constitution for an independent Uganda, Buganda was given its own internal self-government, under the leadership of the kabaka, which was separate from the central government. Former construction worker Milton Obote (1925–2005) formed an alliance between his party, the People's Congress and the Buganda royalist party, *Kabaka*

Yekka ('King Alone') and became Prime Minister while Mutesa II became president. In 1966, Obote amended the constitution, and declared himself president. The following month, the coalition collapsed and the kabaka's palace was attacked, forcing him into exile. The leader of the attack on the palace was Colonel Idi Amin (1925–2003), a former cook in the British Colonial Army who, in 1971, would oust Obote from office and seize power in a military coup.

Independence was always going to be a difficult proposition for Kenyans. From 1952 to 1959 the country was under a state of emergency because of an armed uprising against colonial rule known as the 'Mau Mau' rebellion. From the early part of the twentieth century, Kenya's interior central highlands had been settled by British and European farmers who earned fortunes from farming tea and coffee. By the 1930s, there were around 30,000 but there were also around a million Kikuyu living as itinerant farmers. The white settlers, with a powerful voice in government due to the considerable wealth they brought to the country, introduced laws to prevent these farmers becoming successful competitors, banning them from growing coffee, levying punitive taxes and paying less for their labour.

The Mau Mau revolt started in the 1940s with a campaign of industrial action but the movement had strengthened, with members having to swear ceremonial oaths of loyalty. By the 1950s, the objective of the rebels was to force settlers to abandon their farms and leave Kenya. British forces were brought in from abroad to fight the insurgents and nationalist leaders were arrested. The rebellion, notable for its many atrocities on both sides, had been quashed by 1955 but it had persuaded the British of the injustices perpetrated by the settlers. They accepted the notion of African majority rule in an independent Kenya. Following independence in 1963, nationalist leader Jomo Kenyatta (1894–1978) became first prime minister and then, in 1964, president of the new country.

British Central Africa
In Southern Rhodesia, the white population ruled the black African majority in a similar system to the one operating at the time in South

Africa. While 150,000 of them occupied the best land, the five million Africans in the territory were restricted to the poorest, in about one-third of the country. Pass laws restricted Africans' movement, African political parties were suppressed, and they were permitted only minimal representation in the white-dominated parliament. In 1953, Northern and Southern Rhodesia joined with Nyasaland to form the Federation of Rhodesia and Nyasaland, also known as the Central African Federation, in a deliberate attempt to avert African independence.

African nationalists such as Hastings Banda (1898–1997) of Nyasaland and Harry Nkumbula (1916–1983) of Northern Rhodesia protested to the British government in a letter:

'Of all the Europeans of Central Africa, those of Southern Rhodesia have the worst antipathy towards Africans... They look upon the Africans as inferior beings, with no right to a dignified and refined existence and fit only as hewers of wood and drawers of water for Europeans... It is these Europeans... who will rule and govern the federation... under the Government provided by Southern Rhodesia, the relationship between us and the authorities will be one of slaves and masters, and the cardinal principle... domination.'

(From a memorandum dated 1 May 1949, quoted in *The Rise of Nationalism in Central Africa*, R.I. Rotberg, Harvard, 1962)

Their plea fell on stony ground, however, and the British proceeded with the federation. It was disastrous for Africans who faced wage freezes while the cost of living soared and white settlers enjoyed an economic boom. Strikes were ruthlessly suppressed. Following their attendance at the All-African People's Conference in Accra in 1958, at which members of nationalist movements from all over the continent were present, the Africans' demands increased in volume. The government responded by banning political parties and arresting their leaders. The protests continued unabated.

Finally, in 1960, the British government decided it could no longer support white minority rule in the Central African Federation. In 1963, it was broken up and, in the following year, Nyasaland and Northern Rhodesia became the independent countries of Malawi and Zambia respectively. Little changed in Southern Rhodesia, however, where the white settlers retained control of the country. Many wanted armed struggle but the leader of the Zimbabwe African People's Union (ZAPU), Joshua Nkomo (1917–99), demurred. This led Robert Mugabe (b. 1924), Ndabaningi Sithole (1920–2000) and others to break away from ZAPU and form the Zimbabwe African National Union (ZANU). In 1965, Ian Smith (1919–2007), leader of the white Rhodesia Front Party (RFP), made a Unilateral Declaration of Independence but although the British government under Harold Wilson was angered by Smith's declaration, it did little to stop it. More importantly, the declaration hastened armed confrontation.

'[Ian Smith] made some disastrous political decisions as Prime Minister which directly contributed to the trauma that Zimbabwe is suffering from today... The policies of his Rhodesia Front party radicalised black nationalists and directly spawned the violent and fascist rule of Zanu PF.'

(David Coltart, member of the Zimbabwean Parliament [House of Assembly and Senate] since 2000)

Zimbabwe

Shortly after Smith had proclaimed his Unilateral Declaration of Independence in November 1965, Rhodesian troops clashed for the first time with ZANU guerrillas in northern Rhodesia. More such clashes followed but the rebel groups, ZANU and ZAPU, based in Zambia and Mozambique, were hampered by internecine disputes. In 1975, with guerrillas infiltrating the country and attacking settlers' farms, Robert Mugabe assumed the leadership of ZANU, committing the organisation to socialist revolution. Meanwhile, the Rhodesian army was penetrating deep into Mozambique, attacking villages and destroying the infrastructure in an unsuccessful effort to persuade the FRELIMO government to end its support for ZANU.

Eventually, faced with intense fighting and with his government on the brink of collapse, Smith entered into negotiations in an effort to reach an internal agreement. An election was held and, in June 1979, Bishop Abel Muzorewa (1925–2010), leader of the victorious United African National Council (UANC), became the first prime minister of 'Zimbabwe-Rhodesia'. The police, civil service, and judiciary, however, remained under white control and the guerrillas continued their struggle. By the end of the year, they controlled much of the country and the Smith-Muzorewa government was forced to accept defeat. Later that year, the Lancaster House Agreement was signed in London, at last bringing the civil war to an end.

A subsequent election in 1980 delivered a landslide victory to ZANU, and Robert Mugabe became prime minister of an independent Zimbabwe. He favoured his own Shona clan and immediately started pouring resources into the eastern part of the country where the Shona lived. The rival Ndebele minority was tortured, intimidated and murdered. Mugabe has remained a controversial leader, re-distributing land owned by the white minority to black Zimbabweans. Sanctions were imposed by western governments and Zimbabwe experienced economic difficulties and hyper-inflation from 1998 to 2008. In September 2008, a power-sharing agreement was reached between Mugabe and opposition leader Morgan Tsvangirai (b. 1952), in which Mugabe remained president and Tsvangirai became prime minister. Zimbabwe's economy is now slowly recovering but Mugabe remains the subject of heavy criticism.

Belgian Central Africa

In the late nineteenth century, when King Leopold was first pursuing an African empire, the Belgian government had been unenthusiastic. So, it was with reluctance that it took control of the Congo in 1910. After the Second World War, however, it was just as reluctant to let the colony go. It was no great surprise that some professional Africans began to agitate for reform. In the Congo, Africans were discriminated against at all levels of society, political parties were banned and the colony did not have an independent African newspaper until 1957. Africans did not sit in the Legislative Assembly and they were only employed at the very lowest grades of the civil service. Even education was limited, stopping after primary level. The Belgians relented slightly by allowing some educated Congolese to vote in local elections in 1957. They began to form political parties but these generally represented single ethnic groups and only Patrice Lumumba (1925–61), leader of the *Mouvement National Congolais* (MNC), followed the example of Kwame Nkrumah and Julius Nyerere, attempting to make his MNC a national party.

In 1958, events elsewhere, and especially in neighbouring French Congo-Brazzaville, which was granted independence that year, encouraged politicians in the Belgian Congo to apply pressure for their own independence. The following year, political rallies degenerated into riots and attacks on government buildings, missions and property owned by Europeans. The Belgian government was wary of becoming involved in a costly war of liberation. In January 1960, therefore, to the surprise of all concerned, it offered full political independence within six months. Patrice Lumumba was elected as leader of a very shaky coalition government with Joseph Kasa-Vubu (1910–1969) as the country's first president. But, within a few days, the army had mutinied and the province of Katanga, whose copper mines were the source of much of the country's wealth, had broken away under Moshe Tshombe (1919–69), and declared itself a separate state. The United Nations dispatched a peacekeeping force but it was not permitted to intervene in the secession of Katanga, mainly because of pressure from the United States, suspicious of Lumumba's intentions.

In September 1960, Lumumba was dismissed by President Kasa-Vubu but on 14 September Colonel Joseph Mobutu (1930–97), supported by the American Central Intelligence Agency, staged a military coup. Lumumba escaped house arrest but was captured by troops loyal to Mobutu on 1 December. Shortly after, he was executed by firing squad. In November 1965, Mobutu, now a general, seized power and established strong, central government as president. He made a clean start by re-naming Katanga province 'Shaba' and the country 'Zaire', a name derived from the Portuguese Zaire, an adaptation of the Kongo word *nzere* or *nzadi* – 'the river that swallows all rivers'.

The stories of the independence of the tiny Belgian colonies of Rwanda and Burundi are tales of intense rivalry between the Hutu and the Tutsi. The Tutsi in Rwanda had helped Belgium rule but, when the country achieved independence, the Hutu majority took the opportunity to massacre thousands of Tutsi and drive many more thousands out of the country. The opposite occurred in Burundi where the Tutsi minority took control, massacring many thousands of Hutu.

Portuguese Africa

Compared to the other colonial powers, Portugal was relatively poor and badly needed its colonies, Guinea-Bissau, Cape Verde, Angola and Mozambique. Independence, therefore, was the last thing the Portuguese government was prepared to countenance, and it ruthlessly suppressed protest in each of its territories. The response in Guinea-Bissau and Cape Verde was a war that started in 1963 and lasted until 1973 when independence was declared by the *Partido Africano da Independência da Guiné e Cabo Verde* (PAIGC) led by Cape Verdean agricultural engineer, writer and nationalist Amílcar Cabral (1924–73). Cabral was assassinated in January 1973 before the withdrawal of the Portuguese army eighteen months later. General António de Spínola (1910–96), the Portuguese commander in Guinea-Bissau, concerned at the drain on his country's economy by the wars in Africa, joined with other officers in April 1974 to depose the right-wing Portuguese regime established by António de Oliveira Salazar (1889–1970) which had been in power since 1932. This, in turn, led indirectly to the withdrawal of Portuguese forces from Africa and the subsequent independence of Mozambique and Angola.

Angola was paralysed by war from 1961 to 1975 when independence was finally granted. The main nationalist movement was the *Movimento Popular de Libertação de Angola* (MPLA), founded by Agostinho Neto (1922–79) in 1956 but Holden Roberto's (1923–2007) *Frente Nacional de Libertação de Angola* (FNLA) was also involved in the fighting. Late in the war other movements and external agencies became involved. Chinese-trained Jonas Savimbi's (1934–2002) *União Nacional para a Independência Total de Angola* (UNITA), backed by South Africa, also took up arms against the MPLA. Thus, when the Portuguese withdrew in 1975, Angola was left in a state of civil war. To prevent the MPLA taking control when the country became independent in November 1975, South Africa invaded. Meanwhile, the FNLA was being supplied by the United States and was ready to invade from the north, supported by Zairean troops and mercenaries. Neto and the MPLA assumed control on independence and, by the start of 1976, had expelled the invaders. Although UNITA had been forced to retreat, its troops continued to harass the MPLA government throughout the next decade with South African and American support.

Mozambique achieved independence following the merging of its liberation movements into one organisation, the socialist *Frente de Libertação de Moçambique* (FRELIMO), led by Eduardo Mondlane (1920–69) and his deputy Samora Machel (1933–86). Like the other Portuguese colonies, Mozambique experienced ruthless treatment from its colonial masters. Several hundred protesting peasants were shot dead in the north of the country in June 1960, for example. In 1964, FRELIMO declared war on Portugal but, in 1969, Mondlane was assassinated by a letter bomb. Machel took over and Mozambique eventually achieved independence in 1975, just over a year after Portugal's Carnation Revolution in April 1974. FRELIMO took revenge by giving all Portuguese just twenty-four hours to leave the country and with no more than twenty kilos of luggage.

The Fight for Freedom in Apartheid South Africa

The Union of South Africa, founded in 1910, embraced a wide variety of cultures, ethnicities and races. There was, however, a large European population, the largest population of settlers of any African country. Furthermore, South Africa was the continent's wealthiest country, made rich by the gold mines of the Transvaal and the diamond mines of Kimberley. Investment flowed into the mineral industry and the country's cities grew. In turn, these created a need for businesses to sustain the urban centres with foodstuffs. Agriculture boomed and South Africa enjoyed a vibrant economy.

The paucity of rights enjoyed by Africans before the union, however, was made worse by a government intent on introducing repressive legislation. Africans did not just stand by. The South African Native National Congress – re-named the African National Congress (ANC) in 1925 – advocating political equality for all 'civilised' men – was founded in 1912. The ANC was, in the main, considered to be ineffective and failed to attract the interest of the mass of African workers. It remained distant from other movements such as the APO. It also had little to do with the struggles of the large number of South Asian immigrants in South Africa. They found a leader in a young Indian lawyer named Mohandas K. Gandhi (1869–1948) who, in 1906, launched campaigns of peaceful protest, forcing the government to repeal repressive laws.

Meanwhile, Afrikaner nationalists demanded equality with English for the Afrikaans language and worked to represent poor whites in the countryside and the cities where they faced competition for jobs from blacks and coloureds. This was only exacerbated by soldiers returning from overseas after the First World War. The plummeting price of gold and the high cost of mining resulted in mine owners employing black workers instead of whites as they could pay them less. Tensions rose and segregation was increased, new laws being passed to reinforce segregation in the mines.

In the meantime, South African premier Jan Smuts presided over a period of economic prosperity, his government investing heavily in industry. In 1939, at the outbreak of the Second World War, he persuaded his countrymen to support Great Britain. J.B.M. Hertzog resigned over this, however, and many Afrikaners sympathised with the Germans, especially the Nazi philosophy of racial purity. Nonetheless, South African soldiers fought on the Allied side.

However, as in the First World War, 'Coloured' and African troops were restricted to non-combative roles and prohibited from bearing arms.

During the war, huge numbers of Africans migrated to the cities, rendering the pass system, designed to keep them in rural areas, difficult to enforce. Segregation, too, was impossible to maintain and white South Africans feared for their perceived socially superior status. The National Party came up with a solution – *apartheid* ('apartness' or 'separateness') and apprehensive white South Africans voted them into government. *Apartheid* laws effectively rendered blacks foreigners in most of South Africa. Unless they were in the employ of whites, they were to be restricted to 'reserves' or 'homelands' which were poverty-stricken and overcrowded. The Population Registration Act of 1950 classified people according to race and the Group Areas Act of the same year laid out where the various races were permitted to live. Sexual relations between different races were banned and every aspect of South African life was segregated. Africans were prohibited from forming trade unions and, as a consequence, they earned ten times less than equivalent white workers.

The radical faction of the ANC, led by Walter Sisulu (1912–2003), Oliver Tambo (1917–93) and Nelson Mandela (b. 1918), concluded that holding out for reform was pointless and that fundamental change was needed. The various opposition groups representing Africans joined together to form the Congress Alliance in the 1950s but, in 1956, 156 leaders of the ANC and the other anti-*apartheid* organisations were arrested and charged with high treason. Five years later, all were acquitted but, by then, internal tensions had split the groups, and some ANC members left the organisation to found the Pan-African Congress (PAC). On March 21, 1960, a peaceful demonstration by several thousand PAC members at Sharpeville turned violent and the South African police opened fire, killing 69 demonstrators. Both the ANC and the PAC responded to Sharpeville by deciding that militant insurgency was the only way to achieve their objectives, the ANC developing the manifesto of *Umkhonto we Sizwe* (the Spear of the Nation), its militant wing. In 1962, however, the leaders of both organisations were arrested, convicted of treason and given life sentences to be served on Robben Island in Table Bay. Nelson Mandela made a statement at the opening of his trial which he ended with the famous words:

'During my lifetime I have dedicated myself to the struggle of the African people. I have fought against white domination, and I have fought against black domination. I have cherished the ideal of a democratic and free society in which all persons live together in harmony and with equal opportunities. It is an ideal which I hope to live for and to achieve. But if needs be, it is an ideal for which I am prepared to die.'

Black resentment of the situation did not end, of course, and they began to espouse ideas of black consciousness. Still, protest was always ruthlessly suppressed.

By 1985, the ANC were back and *Umkhonto we Sizwe* guerrillas were engaged in sabotage. The government of P.W. Botha (1916–2006) responded to the increasing violence with even more force than before. In July 1985, he declared a state of emergency and anti-*apartheid* activists were arrested and imprisoned. The damage of these actions to the economy was immense, however, and, as international bankers refused South Africa credit and investors fled the country, the South African economy collapsed. The momentum for change became irresistible and the bans on the ANC, PAC and the South African Communist Party were lifted on 2 February 1990 by President F.W. de Klerk (b. 1936). Trade union restrictions were abolished and political prisoners released, including Nelson Mandela, who had become a symbol of African struggle in South Africa during his twenty-seven years in prison. Negotiations between the ANC and the government led to elections in April 1994 which were won by the ANC. On 10 May 1994, Nelson Mandela was sworn in as President of South Africa 342 years after the Dutch East India Company had founded its settlement at the Cape of Good Hope.

Botswana, Lesotho, Namibia and Swaziland

It was expected by both the British and the South Africans that the British Protectorates of Botswana, Lesotho, Namibia and Swaziland would, in time, be swallowed up by South Africa. As it was, Basutoland and Bechuana were little more than sources of cheap black labour for South Africa and white South Africans already owned much of Swaziland. Chiefs were given responsibility by colonial officials for much of the running of the country but, in the 1950s and 1960s, there was an increasing demand for more democracy. Finally, after the Sharpeville massacre in 1960, Britain abandoned its plans to merge these 'High Commission Territories' with the *apartheid* regime in South Africa. Botswana and Lesotho were granted independence in 1966 and Swaziland in 1968.

Namibia had been governed by South Africa since 1915, even though it was officially a United Nations Trust Territory, the UN version of the League of Nations Mandates. The South Africans had ignored the terms of the Trust, ruling Namibia as if it was a province and failing to prepare it for independence. Thus, in 1960, the South West Africa People's Organization (SWAPO) began a long guerrilla campaign to obtain independence. Namibia would finally achieve it in 1990, but not before South African mining companies had stripped the country of its huge mineral resources.

Africa Since Independence

By 1980, virtually every former colony on the African continent had achieved independence. They were diverse in environment, size and population, tiny states such as Togo, Swaziland and Benin sharing the continent with massive countries like Nigeria and Zaire (former name for the Democratic Republic of the Congo). Outside of South Africa, there was little in the way of industrial development. There were mining industries in Zambia and DR Congo but most of the rest of the continent's new states remained largely agricultural. Ghana, Senegal, Kenya and Uganda enjoyed a successful export trade with their agricultural produce, but farming in other parts of Africa barely rose above subsistence level. As ever, the main export was human labour.

The men who came to power in the early days of independence had fought hard to fulfil their ambitions of establishing and leading sovereign independent nations. Most of them had been educated abroad, although some had emerged from mission schools. Unfortunately, although they had proved adept at rebellion and revolution, when it came to governing a country many of them were found wanting. Some of these towering figures – amongst them Kwame Nkrumah of Ghana, Nnamdi Azikiwe of Nigeria, Leopold Senghor of Senegal and Jomo Kenyatta of Kenya – were swept away to be replaced by men who were perhaps less passionate and less glamorous, but were also more pragmatic in their approach to ruling their countries.

Many of those educated abroad returned home inculcated with socialist or even Marxist doctrines that championed the state's position at the heart of economic development. Socialism, therefore, became the political philosophy of many of the new national governments that had come into being. The euphoric welcome that had been given to independence had created a wealth of unrealistic expectations, promoted to a large extent by the new leaders who promised better jobs and construction of schools, hospitals and transport systems. The economies of the former colonies were hopelessly inadequate, however, and even the provision of basic services proved difficult, let alone employment for all.

Discontent flourished as ordinary people perceived the ruling elite to be little better than previous colonial regimes. The inadequacies of their leaders were felt especially strongly by the new states' often well-educated and professional army officers. In the two decades following Ghana's independence in 1957, there were many military coups, including those in Algeria, Benin, Burkina Faso, Burundi, Chad, Central African Republic, Republic of the Congo, Democratic Republic of the Congo, Ghana, Libya, Mali, Niger, Nigeria, Rwanda, São Tomé and Príncipe, Sierra Leone, Somalia, Sudan, Togo and Uganda. If a country did not have a military government, it was likely to have become an autocratic, single-party state, the exceptions being Botswana, Kenya, Sudan (returned to civilian rule after its military coup) and Tanzania. Meanwhile, the Cold War politics of the United States and the Soviet Union served only to exacerbate the situation, damaging democracy in Africa as they sought to secure their own interests by offering support to African nations.

Often, however, one of the main problems was that the people of the new state felt more loyalty towards their own ethnic grouping or clan than they did to the state and, once the euphoria of ousting colonialism was over, they reverted to those loyalties. Some states – Ghana, Sudan and Zaire – seized all foreign businesses and put Africans in charge, but the inexperienced new managers found it difficult. Corruption became rife and, in many countries, became the norm. States invested in industry, believing that to be the way to achieve the type of wealth enjoyed by European nations, but it was inefficient and, more often than not, it failed. Meanwhile, state management of agriculture was reminiscent of the way the colonial authorities had governed and bred dissent. Most aspects of life were controlled from the centre and systems of patronage developed in which friends and relatives of those in government benefited from new projects. Those in power held control of all the revenue flooding into their countries, whether it was resources from foreign countries, humanitarian organisations or international businesses. The institutions of state were in disarray and only bribery, corruption and intimidation worked.

In those first years after the wave of independence began, there were also bloody conflicts brought about by secessionist movements in Sudan, Nigeria and the Congo. It was not long, however, before the fragile condition of the new states' economies, the flagrant human rights abuses that were perpetrated in many of them by a ruling class that clung to power by violent means, and the failure of many of the expensive development projects that had been undertaken, led to a fresh wave of African independence movements in the mid-1970s.

Decades of Crisis

In the final decades of Africa's turbulent twentieth century, the continent faced grave problems, the two biggest of which were international debt and drought. The adverse trade terms established during the colonial period were compounded by the lavish spending of governments immediately following independence. The price of the continent's raw material exports dropped drastically in relation to that of imported manufactured goods. Governments ran out of foreign exchange and were forced to turn for help to the International Monetary Fund (IMF) and the World Bank just to pay off the interest on existing loans, loans that they had no hope of ever repaying. The repayment of these debts brought huge problems. The sets of preconditions – Structural Adjustment Programmes – required borrowing governments to balance their budgets which usually meant cuts in public spending that led to a hike in unemployment and even more poverty. Worse than that, however, was devaluation. This meant a rise in the price of exported goods but the prices of imports also rose and these were essentials such as fuel, oil and food to feed the populations of Africa's growing cities.

The precondition of liberalisation of capital controls also did little to help. After independence, countries with little or no capital of their own had set restrictions on the movement of capital, so that profits remained within the country. In the 1980s and 1990s, foreign investors were permitted to take their profits and their capital out of the country as they wished. Most sub-Saharan countries were in Structural Adjustment Programmes by the early 1990s and international money-men were more concerned that Africa paid off its debts by increasing exports than by becoming self-sufficient. Farmers and pastoralists suffered due to the concentration on cash crops rather than food crops. Astonishingly, in some places, while the population starved, international banks were still being paid their interest.

Apart from debt, the other enduring problem was, and still is, drought. In the period following independence, Africa enjoyed higher-than-average rainfall which led to an increase in agricultural production. This was followed, however, by a drought that lasted twenty years through the 1970s and 1980s. Of course, Africans have, in the past, dealt often with climate change and, in the 1990s, there was a growing awareness amongst governments of the need to develop local solutions to their problems.

The oil crisis of 1973, when the Organisation of Petroleum-Exporting Countries (OPEC) suspended oil shipments to countries that had supported Israel in the Arab-Israeli War of October 1973, did not help. The price of oil quadrupled and, with forty African countries being net importers of oil, it was a disaster for the continent. Transport became prohibitively expensive and the prices of African exports became, consequently, uncompetitive. Thus, the price of imported food rose, making it accessible only to the wealthy elite.

In May 1963, thirty-two African heads of state founded the Organisation of African Unity (OAU) (re-named the African Union in 2002) to promote political and economic cooperation between African states. Some have criticised it for having no teeth and being little more than a 'talking shop', and others, calling it 'The Dictators' Club', have claimed that it did little to protect the rights of African citizens from their own leaders. It has remained intact, however, working with the United Nations to ease the problems of refugees and creating the African Development Bank to promote economic projects and free former colonial nations from reliance on finance from their one-time colonial masters or other foreign countries. The African Union now consists of fifty-three member states.

By the end of the 1980s, Africa was crippled by foreign debt, its inhabitants were experiencing a steadily worsening standard of living, and drought and famine stalked the land from the Horn of Africa to the Sahel and Southern Africa. As if that was not bad enough, a new killer arrived on the scene that was to sweep through the continent – the dreadful scourge of AIDS.

Africa in the 21st Century

Africa is now made up of fifty four sovereign nations, most of them still demarcated by the borders created by the colonial powers. In the main, they are republics, operating under a presidential system. Most have experienced difficulty in maintaining democratic governments and many have experienced military dictatorships, these often coming to power as a result of instability brought about by ethnic or territorial conflicts.

Two thousand years ago, sub-Saharan Africa's population is estimated to have been around a fifth of that of China and, in the following centuries, this ratio continued to decline. By 1900, the population of Africa accounted for just one per cent of the world's population. During the twentieth century, however, and especially over the last sixty years, Africa's population grew rapidly, from 221 million in 1950 to a billion in 2009. Consequently, it is a young population; in some states more than half the people are aged under twenty-five.

At the start of the twenty first century, many of the world's poorest countries were located in Africa. Average income per capita is lower than it was at the end of the nineteen sixties and half the population lives on around $1.25 a day. Access to education still lags behind the world's other nations, there is high child mortality and one African in five lives in a country that is seriously disrupted by warfare. With the information revolution providing employment and revenue around the world, Africa is in danger of being left behind yet again. Meanwhile, investment has fled the continent and its share of exports in traditional primary products has fallen.

Colonialism brought a great many evils, of course, but one benefit was the understanding and eradication of killer diseases such as yellow fever, river blindness and polio. There is also knowledge of the source and means of transmission of parasitical diseases such as sleeping sickness, bilharzia, kala-azar and malaria, although the latter, still claiming a huge number of African lives, continues to defeat scientists searching for a vaccine. The arrival of HIV AIDS in the last two decades of the twentieth century has affected Africa, where it is believed to have originated, more than anywhere else in the world, especially Sub-Saharan Africa. In 2007, it was estimated that 68% of all people living with the disease are located there while 76% of all deaths from AIDS occur there. Now the largest cause of death in the region, it is threatening to cut life expectancy in Africa by twenty years. It also undermines development and growth in many countries as well as doing untold damage to the social fabric of the continent.

Conflict, too, has claimed millions of lives, the most serious being the Second Congo War that was fought between 1998 and 2003 in the Democratic Republic of the Congo (formerly Zaire). Considered the deadliest conflict since the Second World War, it involved eight African nations and around twenty-five armed groups. 5.4 million people died in the war and, as a result of it, most of them from disease and starvation. In Rwanda, a civil war ended with genocide in 1994 in which Hutu extremists are estimated to have killed up to a million Tutsi. And there have been countless other conflicts in Africa since independence, more than twenty in this century alone. A conflict in Darfur waged by the Sudanese government against the non-Arab indigenous population has created a humanitarian crisis of huge proportions.

Famine, too, has claimed the lives of millions in the last century and continues to be a major killer in the current one. Since 2000, there have been several famines. Niger has experienced a food crisis caused by an early end to the 2004 rains, endangering 2.4 million people. Famine in the Sahel in 2010 resulted from erratic rains in the 2009–2010 growing season, while the Horn of Africa is currently being affected by a severe drought affecting more than thirteen million people.

Agriculture remains the dominant factor in the African economy, with 80 per cent of all Africans involved in cultivation or pastoralism. The continent's mineral resources continue to be mined but only provide a living for a small percentage of Africans. Another resource found underground, oil, has become a major source of revenue for nineteen African states.

All is not lost, however. Child mortality rates, although high, are declining. Deaths of mothers during child-birth declined by 26 per cent between 1990 and 2009 and the number of people living in extreme poverty, although it is also high, is declining. In 1980, just 28 per cent of Africans lived in cities. Today that figure has risen to 40 per cent. Of course, urbanisation of this kind can create poverty and slum-dwelling, but it can also boost productivity with workers moving from agricultural labour into urban employment, leading to increased demand and greater investment.

The Arab Spring

On 18 December 2010, in the rural town of Sidi Bouzid, Tunisian street vendor Mohamed Bouazizi set himself on fire in protest at perpetual harassment by local police officers who told him he required a licence to sell his wares on the street. As he lacked the funds to bribe the relevant officials, his goods were confiscated. He subsequently poured a can of petrol over himself and lit it outside the office of the town's governor. He died just over two weeks later and became the focal point for protests in Tunisia that were the first in the phenomenon known as the 'Arab Spring', a series of sustained protest campaigns across the Arab world.

Up to September 2011, these popular uprisings, often organised using social media, have removed three North African heads of state from office. Tunisia's President Zine El Abidine Ben Ali (born 1936) who had been in office for twenty-four years, fled to Saudi Arabia on 14 January 2011; and Egypt's President Hosni Mubarak (born 1928), who had been in office for thirty years, resigned on 11 February 2011, after eighteen days of mass protests and a state of emergency in his country that had lasted for decades. Meanwhile, after ruling for forty two years, Libyan leader Muammar Gaddafi was overthrown when, on 20 August, 2011, the opposition Libyan National Liberation Council seized control of the military compound of Bab al-Azizia in the southern suburbs of Tripoli. Gaddafi was controversially shot dead two months later in his home town of Sirte. Several other leaders, such as Sudanese President Omar al-Bashir, have announced that they will not seek re-election when their term of office ends.

The issues that have led to these demonstrations are many and various – dictatorial leadership, human rights violations and government corruption have been cited, alongside economic factors such as increasing food prices, unemployment and poverty. The participants came from all levels of society, both men and women, but large numbers of disaffected youth played an important role. Ultimately, the increased availability of education and the consequent rise in aspiration, faced with a corresponding absence of the desire for reform on the part of incumbent governments, is largely responsible for these revolts.

The New 'Scramble for Africa'

Sixty years on from the beginnings of independence for African states, the phenomenon of colonisation seems set to return, albeit in a subtler form. Indeed, it has been dubbed a 'new scramble for Africa' but, in reality, its aims are exactly the same as the nineteenth century scramble – the denuding of the continent of its mineral riches. Africa has become the front line of a battle for control of the world's oil and gas resources.

Many large corporations have been accused of facilitating corruption and even provoking instability in order to enter into deals with African leaders that are far from beneficial to their countries. These corporations from the United States, Britain, France and China are now competing for the favours of chaotic regimes that very often function against a backdrop of bribery and corruption. Gas, diamonds and especially oil, of which Africa is thought to have 15 per cent of the world's total reserves, are the objectives of these arrangements but there are accusations of money being siphoned into financial 'black holes' in Europe. Banks are making enormous, multibillion dollar loans in exchange for future oil rights; effectively, a country's future prosperity is being sold off cheap.

Naturally, this has produced a boom in some African countries and the marked increase in foreign investment – it tripled between 2000 and 2005 – is welcome. China's consumption of oil has doubled in the last decade and it has turned to Africa to provide it. Moreover, Chinese trade with Africa has increased tenfold in a decade, mostly with oil-producing states such as Sudan, Nigeria and Angola. However, China is also involved in mining in Zambia, Namibia and South Africa.

It remains to be seen what impact this wooing of Africa will have on the continent, whether any of the subsequent prosperity will trickle down to the ordinary people. It never has in the past but to create successful industry takes stability and peace. Perhaps those involved will place a value on that, rather than choose once again to take the money and run, leaving ordinary Africans to live in poverty and despair.

Further Reading

Ade Ajayi, J.F. (ed.), *UNESCO General History of Africa volume 6: Africa in the Nineteenth Century Until the 1880s*, Oxford: James Currey, 1992

Adu Boahen, A. (ed.), *UNESCO General History of Africa volume 7: Africa under Colonial Domination 1880–1935*, Oxford: James Currey, 1990

Curtain, Philip; Feierman, Steven; Thompson, Leonard; Vansina, Jan, *African History: From Earliest Times to Independence*, Harlow, Middlesex: Addison Wesley Longman, 1996

Dowden, Richard, *Africa: Altered States, Ordinary Miracles*, London: Portobello Books, 2009

Fage, John D., *A History of Africa*, London: Routledge, 2001

Hrbek, I. (ed.), *UNESCO General History of Africa volume 3: Africa from the 7th to the 11th Century,* Oxford: James Currey, 1992

Isichei, Elizabeth, *A History of African Societies to* 1870, Cambridge: Cambridge University Press, 1997

Ki-Zerbo, J., (ed.) *UNESCO General History of Africa volume 1: Methodology and African Prehistory*, Oxford: James Currey, 1990

Ki-Zerbo, J., and Niane, D.T. (ed.) *UNESCO General History of Africa Volume 4: Africa from the Twelfth to the Sixteenth Century*, Oxford: James Currey, 1997

Mazrui, A.A., (ed.) *UNESCO General History of Africa volume 8: Africa since 1935. Unabridged paperback: Africa Since 1935*, Oxford: James Currey, 1994

Meredith, Martin, *The State of Africa*, London: The Free Press, 2005

Mokhtar, G. (ed.) *UNESCO General History of Africa volume 2: Ancient Civilizations of Africa: Ancient Civilizations of Africa,*

Oxford: James Currey, 1990

Ogot, B.A. (ed.) *UNESCO General History of Africa volume 5: Africa from the 16th to the 18th Century*, Oxford: James Currey, 1999

Reader, John, *Africa: A Biography of the Continent*, London: Penguin, 1998

Reid, Richard J., *History of Modern Africa*, London: Wiley-Blackwell, 2008

Shillington, Kevin, *History of Africa*, London: Macmillan Education, 1995

Index